A BLOODIED TAPESTRY

*THE AMERICAN WAR
IN VIETNAM FROM A
CIVILIAN WAR VETERAN'S
PERSPECTIVE*

JANSTEPHEN JAMES
CAVANAUGH, PH.D.

Copyright © 2022 JanStephen James Cavanaugh

All rights reserved. No part of this publication in print or in electronic format may be reproduced, stored in a retrieval system, or transmitted in any form or by any means, electronic, mechanical, photocopying, recording, or otherwise without the prior written permission of the publisher.

The scanning, uploading, and distribution of this book without permission is a theft of the author's intellectual property. Thank you for your support of the author's rights.

Design and distribution by Bublish, Inc.
Published by Age of Peace 2050 Project

ISBN: 978-1-647045-11-1 (eBook)
ISBN: 978-1-647045-12-8 (paperback)

Caveat

The muse fashioned the themes of sex and violence, the "red threads" of my story, as written. No complaints about the details of violence. **Do be forewarned there have been some complaints about** the details of sex in a story about war. Unnecessary, "distractor," "TMI" too personal, and those same people judged it a "brilliant story," "well written," like watching a movie.

Maybe I needed to change what is written?

So, what to do? The writer in me asserts, "The way the story is told, is what is to be told." Do I trust the muse and keep the story "As Written?" Do I bow to the wishes of some and greatly mute or remove the objectionable parts of my story?

I have talked to friends and advisors. I have wrestled with my placating self. I have imagined eliminating or modifying the offending scenes and when I do so my gut strongly tightens in resistance. Did you know our human gut is the largest source of synapses outside our human brain; our first brain. Life lesson: how many times did my gut speak clearly, and I did not listen. With deep regrets.

Best I understand the reason for sex in a story about war is the sense of aliveness against the backdrop of violence. Eros and Thanatos from my early boyhood to early manhood.

For better or worse, I am sure you will tell me, I will leave it "As Written."

JanStephen

Introduction

Civilian Perspective, American War in Vietnam, II Corps, South Vietnam, 1967–1969

My story draws from a well of personal journals written during my time in war as a civilian. Journaling is a habit I started in Catholic seminary and unwittingly gives witness to my story.

What is written herein is a series of essays that interweaves a tapestry of memories that crisscross my time in South Vietnam from 1967 to 1969. The "American War," as the Vietnamese have named it.

JanStephen James Cavanaugh, PhD

Prologue

The price I paid for getting my "war nerves" in Vietnam from 1967 to 1969 was not evident to me until 1990. As part of my professional training in treating war trauma, I was attending a PTSD workshop. I remember listening to the story of a navy medic, a veteran of Vietnam. Suddenly out of the blue it hit me: his story was my story.

He was telling his story about how he had been so long in denial. He all these years suffered disordered sleep undiagnosed because he thought himself "a lowly medic" and not worthy of war stress disorders. As a lowly civilian in that war, my body heaved in grief as I wept in recognition. From then on, I identified myself as a Civilian Vietnam War Veteran.

This was the beginning of being able to tell the story that I now invite you to read. A story that contains the normal struggles of my life: my high idealism and the terrifying realism of war, of loving friendship and of deep betrayal. Nothing that unusual or fantastical...but it's my story just the same.

I know that the writing of this story is more about my needing to tell it, and I'm not sure why. In truth, I do hope the story will create a sympathetic view of "the enemy," which most often starts from within. To love and to forgive ourselves and others for our participation in "bad times" past. Each side was fighting for their cherished beliefs, and as a principle of war, committed to getting the killing done as quickly as possible.

War philosophers predict that misuse of the principles of war leads to unending and unwinnable wars. We observed violations of these principles in our time. Predicting wars could end badly. And they did. Many of our generals betrayed us. Sold out to the military industrial complex. Eisenhower warned us.

I am as guilty of participating in the sins of war as anyone else.

As a way of healing from the pain of war, I imagine each side offering apologies for the horrible deeds and atrocities committed. Confession is good for the collective soul. War is barbarism. Such a reconciliation would go a long way to healing the psychic wound still at the core of the American/Vietnamese relationship. We are beautiful peoples who need to heal the wounds of war.

And I do see that taking place…I read stories of old enemies meeting in peace on former battle fields in mutual respect, old soldiers on both sides eating and drinking in good company.

June 27, 2021
JanStephen James Cavanaugh

Contents

Caveat	iii
Introduction	v
Prologue	vii
JanStephen James Cavanaugh	1
Harpers Ferry, June–July 1967	15
Philippines, July 1967	23
Saigon, August 1967	29
Reflections Based on Journal Notes, Summer and Fall '67	33
Kon Tum, August 1967	39
Nha Trang Language Study, September 1967	49
Kon Tum, Winds of War, October–November 1967	53
A Siesta Visitor, November 1967	69
Purple Heart Incident, Late Fall 1967	73
Preview Tet, January 1968	75
January 3, 1968, Kon Tum	77
1/10/1968	79

Commentary on Journal Entry, January 14, 1968	81
Letters to Luisa, Tet '68	83
Post Tet 1968, Transition from International Voluntary Services to Catholic Relief Services	89
I Destroyed It to Save It	91
Renata Captured	93
May 15, 1968, North of Kon Tum	95
Deep Agent, Fred	97
Recollections: Minh Quy Hospital and Jeff	101
Random Memories of Vietnam, 1967–1969	105
Spring 1969	109
Civilian Vietnam War Veteran	115
Epilogue	117

JanStephen James Cavanaugh

I was born at Royal Victoria Hospital, Barrie, Ontario, Canada, June 10, 1943. A WWII baby.

I was raised in a farmhouse on eighth concession Vespra Township, Simcoe County. Primitive living by today's standards. Electricity was irregular; so often we had light by lamp. Water carried in from the well house, which sat on the fence line of the barnyard. Outhouse outback. Carrying water and emptying the chamber pot was one of my first responsibilities. I can still remember what a wonderful thing it was to have running water, even if not yet hot water except from heating it on the wood stove.

An early formative memory: I am no more than age five, standing in front of the farm kitchen stove, the only source of heat on a blustery winter's day. I can feel the heat through my heavy winter clothing, giving me a head start before heading off into the cold. I can still feel the snow cap fur round my face. I can hear the wind whistle through the window cracks. Mother is dressing me to go outside in the bitter cold with Dad. I can see him standing there, also by the stove, getting ready to go and dig the quicksand out of the water trough. In our artesian well-water, there is a fine gray quicksand. This the only source of water for the cattle. If you did not periodically remove this fine gray sand, the trough would fill up with quicksand and be of no use for the cattle to drink. I remember mom looking me in the eye and saying, "You are the farmer." Much too young to dig the heavy gray sand, but with a small snow shovel in hand standing atop a high snow drift, I dig keeping pace with my dad. I look down at him shoveling the stuff so heavy while the wind and snow are so fierce. I can still feel it biting my face. Digging quicksand on a bitter day is a matter of life and death, and I am learning that lesson.

By circumstance of birth, I was the first-born male in a Roman Catholic family of seven siblings. I would have been a third-generation farmer. As far as I understand how the money works, usually by third generation the land is paid for, and there's good soil that's been farmed well, with the prosperity to buy better and produce more. I could have been a millionaire farmer by now. Maybe several. But that was not my path. I do have my sorrows, and my sins have been a means to bring more meaning and honesty to my life. And I ask forgiveness for my failures in love. They are many.

The impetus to leave my destiny as a farmer came to me in a dream. That dream and other factors put me on a path to priesthood that brought me to the United States of America in 1963.

My last evening on the farms in South Ontario was spent doing what I loved most: working the land with machines. I was bailing the straw from oat harvest on an early September evening. I can still see in my mind's eye myself seated on tractor, my head turned right (so much so, so much of the time that as an old man I have more arthritis on right side) to monitor the baler. The sun was glowing hot red in the cloudless blue western sky, which made seeing hard. The hills of Collingwood felt very much like the distant mountains outside my window in West Hurley, New York, a purple line against the brilliant late summer sun. The smell of fresh bailed straw mixed with the sound of the slightly modulating RPM from a purring English Ford three-cylinder diesel engine responding to the plunger action of the John Deere baler. Pick up straw, push, crunch, cut, repeat: each bale slowly emerged inches at a time like birth. Up and down the wind row we go. It was easy work for both driver and engine; together we sweated and growled our way through planting and harvesting. The puffs of dust of plunger action refracted though the setting sun and cloaked the earth with a golden halo. Beauty. Motion. Stillness.

In a few hours, I would be on a bus to Chicago, United States, heading toward a seminary for Roman Catholic priests. I was totally unprepared for the journey. Blissfully unaware that early fall evening, lost in doing what I loved to do.

The Peace before the Struggle.

God has given me these moments when time stands still and another reality manifests. Moments more real than reality. They are moments of awed beauty, and upon occasion, of awed fright.

I was given a great gift of love. My mother, Theresa, could not marry for love. She was a Catholic in love with non-Catholic airman in a time of war, and her mother forbade it. So, if not for love, then she would live her life her way in a man's world. Though a city girl, she decided to marry into a Catholic farm family. With this mindset, she met my father, and the rest is history. I never asked her why Stephen my baptismal name.

Many, many years later my mother revealed to me in very personal conversations about times past. I was the lead son who showed promise and ability, and she had many gifted sons. And beautiful daughters too, in hopes of marrying into farmland. She had visions of a farm dynasty, "like *Dynasty* on TV," she said. Without protest, she gave up her dream of a dynasty to allow her son his dream. No greater love has a mother. It brings to mind Bernini's *The Ecstasy of St. Teresa* in Cornaro Chapel, Santa Maria della Vittoira, Rome, Italy. The expression on her face is of pure bliss, a heart penetrated by love. To be in the presence of that statue is to be in one of my favorite places in the whole world. My mother, Theresa, was that to me.

From early on, I remember feeling this "soft spot" for something called God, a very warm presence near my heart. I did feel a "call" to lead a celibate life, although it seems strange to admit it as we live in a world that judges such as odd and neurotic.

I remember one experience at age seven, at evening "fall supper" at schoolhouse, watching boys excitedly running after shrieking girls, having fun feeling them up in a game of chase. I was certainly curious as to what their fingers were feeling, and then a voice strong from behind me said right in my ear, "You are not like other boys dominated by your penis." That voice marked me.

These men in black cassocks would visit us on the farm. Before I had words for such a thing, I desired to be one of them. My interest would seem strange to an observer of my childhood, given the negative feelings about the Church hierarchy within my Catholic family, still stinging from the betrayal by the Church in Ireland. My mother loved the Church's rituals and sacraments; the Mass is special to her. She did not think well, though, of priests or bishops. Sort of a necessary annoyance. Even though my parents assigned me as "farmer," they quietly resigned to give up first-born son to the Church.

The part of English Canada where I lived was seriously anti-Catholic in my youth. In 1926, the KKK bombed Barrie, Ontario's St. Mary's Roman Catholic Church[1]. The family lore is the bomb would have killed my great grandparents if it had not gone off early. Maybe planned that way, but either way I was constantly chided for a religion in which men wore skirts. And some would pick a fight, egged on by their contemporaries. Repeatedly.

I know what it is like to be a minority. To avoid being bullied, fighting Protestants became a way of life in those early years. The physical conditioning of a farm life and a gift of very quick reflexes helped me win most of them. I also learned quickly that there is always somebody bigger, stronger, and quicker. You did not have to win; you just had to make him hurt enough to leave you alone. I grew up in a culture in which violence, and to be violent, was an expected part of manly life. That was what earned respect and the girls.

Through the eyes of my childhood these men in black were good men, reminding us that there was more to life than working, drinking, fighting, and fucking. They taught that it was not right for husbands to ill-treat their wives and children. The "love your enemy" injunction was hard to grasp given my circumstances, posing a challenge to my faith. And I know my Church is as misogynistic as it gets, but that is not the whole story. Steps in time to gender

---

[1] "Remember This? The Ku Klux Klan would forever regret their expansion into the Town of Barrie," BarrieToday.com, https://www.barrietoday.com/columns/remember-this/remember-this-the-klu-klux-klan-would-forever-regret-their-expansion-into-the-town-of-barrie-561190, 15 Mar 2017.

equality. Marriage makes a sacrament to protect women from the violence and abuse of men. Monastic traditions empowered women, nuns being the original feminists.

I saw these men as dedicating themselves by lifestyle to "higher things." I admired them even with and sometimes because of their weaknesses. I could not speak these words then. I felt drawn to that way of life, and then, a life changing dream at age fourteen put the seal on the deal. In the dream, I get out of bed, and I stand before a second story bedroom window of our Stewart[2] farmhouse, looking out. To my right at a few hundred feet and what ought to have been the neighbor's farmhouse, I see a figure of a small boy standing on a hilltop. The early dawn sun is just up, and I know the boy is me. I see him poised, looking off in the distance, watching the golden domes of the city shining in morning light, knowing that is where he is headed.

---

[2] Mom and Dad had bought more land, and the Stewart farm was considered one of the best farms in the valley.

A long stick and attached bag are all his possessions over his shoulder, dressed in a style of long ago. Still in dream state, I hear a noise, and I step closer to the window. Looking to my left in what should have been the bull's pasture, I see monastery's wall up close, the stones so beautifully gray and well mortared. I fall in love with the sight of the wall. What draws me forward? I am enchanted by the sound of monk's chant coming from within. As I hear the sound, I feel my heart's energy being sucked inside. I want to be inside to be one of them, the dream so real.

I can still feel that sucking feeling some sixty years later. The Purity of Love in prayer. Oh, the ache in my heart. That longing deep to be inside. Instead, the little boy on the hill, perhaps left on the doorstep and raised by the monks, now by the abbot sent out into the world. At least that is how I make sense of the dream—a prefiguring of an event that would occur later and reshape my life.

The dream stirred deep longings for priestly life and such an exquisite pain in knowing that love existed. Wanting to be part of making a more compassionate world that was possible if we would love each other. I wanted to be one of them.

Catholicism gave me a belief about what is possible if humans would love one another. It is a great teaching from such a very human institution bearing the sins of humanity two thousand plus years old. I understand the soft underbelly of the Church and certainly saw this side in Vietnam. The seven sins visit all men and all women in all manners of power! To me, this is part of the natural order of things, the outcome of our original sin. And why justice must prevail so that things do not become violently unnatural unto war. True justice is a measure of love. We all exist in a state of sin, each of us committing an original sin. An original decision in a moment to break from love! This is why there is the need for confession, forgiveness, and redemption.

My United States destination was Glen Ellyn, Illinois where I was to enroll in undergraduate studies for priesthood in the Catholic Foreign Mission Society of America—Maryknoll. The Society's namesake is the Mary mother of Jesus, Mother of God as spoken in the Mass. Her assumption to be crowned Queen of Heaven an Immutable Truth. That all this is so about Mary confounds even believers and is part of what I like about my faith. The story of love goes into deep mythology (truth-bearing stories a la Joseph Campbell) to get us out of ego mind and into the land of soul experience. I thought of Maryknoll as a kind of foreign legion ideal focused on the domain of love. I carried (and often prayed with) my rosary beads on my person throughout Vietnam.

I can now see the foreign legion motif fits well the story I tell.

I completed my studies at Glen Ellyn and obtained a BA in scholastic philosophy in May of 1966. My thesis was on Eidetic Reduction and Husserl. When combined with math, science, logic, debate, language, history, theology, literature, and lots of philosophy, it made for a lot of fun and hard work: it was a great education. Our Church provides its best with the best of education.

In between undergraduate and graduate training for priesthood is novitiate. I notified my parents of my decision to continue into novitiate in spring of '66. They responded by selling the family farms. None of my brothers or sisters were interested in the land, and with no hope of my return, my father and mother had no desire to continue what had become quite a large operation. My mother's dream of dynasty was over.

Dad was forced onto the land by his father, who put his sons on farms as alternate "duty" during WWII. They worked to provide food to keep armies marching. My dad never wanted to be a farmer. He loved music and played big band drummer. He used to practice. He loved to watch great drummers on television and imitate them. He was good. He always talked of being a barber, but for all his reluctance, he was a very progressive farmer. He believed it good that farmers have a union and have some say in the pricing. This is where I get the roots of my "liberal" bend of thinking. He was willing to try new ideas and was quite successful at farming.

For example, our farm was plagued by a weed we called "yellow rocket." Fast growing, it destroyed all in its path. It was so serious that the local provincial agriculture agent came to our one-room eighth grade schoolhouse one afternoon. He recruited the older students to take the afternoon off, and we went to my farm fields. We all went in large numbers to pull, one by one, this deadly weed from the ground. Mrs. Wattie, our teacher, agreed. Seems odd now for such a thing to happen. Truly neighbor helping neighbor to protect themselves. I do recall being in the fields with my schoolmates, picking weed bundles and putting them on piles to burn. I can still see the bundles burning and feeling good about the field cleared of this destructive weed. The best part of the day was "pop" and ice cream afterward.

After that event, my father invested in weed sprayer to fit hydraulic arms on the back of his tractor. He was the first farmer in the valley to do that. Fifteen-foot swaths of liquefied 2,4-D in just the right measure is far faster than fifteen people pulling weeds. It's the miracle of science. Ever the businessman, Dad became the custom sprayer for crops throughout the valley. I can still taste the 2,4-D from using my mouth to blow out plugged up nozzles. Even with the X-rated warnings on the five-gallon cans, none of us really knew the dangers. The power to kill weeds so easily and quickly is a wonderful thing. Mother tells of Dad smelling of 2,4-D in bed even after he bathed. I wonder if this may have played a role in his death.

After the sale of the farms, my parents moved to Barrie, Ontario. Dad pursued a career in farm real estate, with much success.

My own part in their farm story is that I returned to Canada in June of 1966 to assist with the sale of the farms. I returned to the states a month later for advanced summer studies in Protestant theology at the University of San Francisco. In fall of '66, I entered novitiate in Hingham, Massachusetts.

Novitiate is a "year of trial." The focus is on spiritual development as the candidate "puts together" his priesthood. The foundation is not just thinking about it but doing the spiritual practices of priesthood. For sure there was a structure of daily prayers and meetings and parish projects. But once left more to your own devices, what does one do with one's time and energy?

In my view, everyone should have some kind of novitiate before undertaking life-long vows. It is a time to reflect, to be with oneself, and to figure out if you have what it takes to do what your vows are intending.

There were many positives of that year, but mostly, it was a year of trial indeed. A crisis of faith occurred when sensing I might not have what they wanted, and I began to make alternate plans. All was resolved by the end of year "review" of my candidacy. My first level vows were in the balance. Each candidate's review was overseen by Maryknoll's Mother House in Ossining, NY. The word came down, and I was asked to leave. Not on unfriendly grounds—told I was too much a "loner" and suggested that I have some time to think it over. At least two years.

And they were right. There was too much Karl Jung in my understanding of Catholic teachings, and maybe as a Jesuit, I would have made it, I wonder. I have often thought if ordained, I would be sent to South America in Ronald Reagan's time, when local government sponsored terrorists trained by the US[3] military tortured and killed priests and raped and killed nuns. Given the bend of my thinking, I was likely to be one of them.

As life would have it, during that year I had also fallen deeply in love. Luisa. And although I was not yet ready to make a commitment to her, my heart and body felt committed even though I would be far away. And she much the same. In 1970 I immigrated to the USA and made her my wife and the love of my life. And other wonderful loves as well.

But back then...what to do with my newfound freedom now that returning to the farms in Canada was no longer an option? I wanted to do something different. I needed to get away to foreign lands. My studies had given me a view of the world beyond farming. Perhaps because of the feeling of the Kennedy era and certainly for reasons and motivations related to my background, I joined International Voluntary Services (IVS). They would take me as a "third country national." IVS was an organization whose mission, in so many ways, was just a continuation of my seminary training, broadly defined as "human development."

IVS would send me to be a farmer in a foreign land. Farming was my first love, as already noted. Even today in spring, the smell of freshly turned soil and in summer, the earthy smell of mowed hay and the beautiful sound and the sweet smell of engine running hard and burning clean flood my senses even now.

I started farmyard chores at age six, milking cows. One cow a day, "Blackie," and it was only evening milking at first. Then with each year, the list grew: morning milking and then three cows then more, and a host of other "chores" associated with mixed farming[4]. Daily chores in the

---

[3] Fort Benning Georgia, formerly known as the School of Americas.
[4] cows, calves, steers, pigs, and chickens.

barns morning and night were a way of life. As the oldest, I had to lead the way. And to be sure, the shoveling of a lot of shit—the best way to describe manure—became imprinted on my mind. The stuff that gives life to life. So much time milking by hand, and my fingers wrapped around hard to steer steering wheel of tractors, and tightly gripping the handle, forking hay and shoveling shit, that my finger development became misshapen. My hands were shaped by hard work while my bones were still growing. Lifting so hard that my right arm, with the constant pull on the muscle, elongated my elbow, and later in life needed surgery to fix.

Much to my city girl mother's married farmer horror, I started driving tractor at age ten. Instead of learning about harnessing horses as farm boys of previous generations did, in my generation of farmers, the big change was engines to do the pulling and pushing. They were cantankerous…not always wanting to start. Seems they had personalities.

My first memory of driving tractor goes like this: It is evening after supper and rather than do milking I am seated on the flat bed seat of Allis Chalmers B tractor. I can see the sun set low in the west. I'm not yet strong enough to push the heavy spring-loaded clutch in and let it out slowly enough not to stall. To my left, I can see my father standing by the big drive wheel, talking to me. Above the engine noise I follow, and I can see the gear numbers imprinted like an "H" casting an orange color next to the shifter. I am in second gear of three gears and one reverse, down to the left. The throttle level is notched at one-quarter. Once going I push the throttle up to three-quarters. Then my father starts running alongside, just in  front of big drive wheel, his arms stretching to release the clutch. Off I go, casting an over the shoulder glance at my mother standing in the woodshed door with her mouth open. It's springtime, and the fields are to be harrowed to open the very wet soil to the sun. His injunctions clear, Dad watches the gauges, oil, water, and battery, emphasizing the importance of oil pressure if the oil pump blows, I am to push the stop button quick, or the engine dies quick. He also makes me aware of a small rectangular box on the steering column, with little round glass enclosed voltmeter and two buttons: one left for night lights to pull out and one button to the right to push in to stop. Avoid muddy patches and stay out of the deep ditch on west roadside. I do good, and maybe that evening, the tractor and I fall in love.

After that, I quickly developed the strength to clutch. The amount of clutching caught up with me in old age...made my left knee a problem. I would spend thousands of hours driving tractors over the next decade. Tractors big and small, in weather wet and hot and cold, and I loved it all. I drove tractors like no other. I understood their limits, and I could make them dance.

Some ask, "Do you feel abused by early farm life?" No. For sure I faced hard labor from an early age, made more so by my father's illnesses. I saw it as my duty as oldest son to do what needed to be done, without really thinking about it. Be responsible, that's the way it was. Always on farms, children are put to work to learn the skills of farming, which are best learnt by observing and hands on practice. No abuse of any kind; my parents never laid a hand on me. My mother's "look" was enough. She shouted at me once or twice, and for good reason. I was a good and sensitive boy. Not easy to be me when boys are supposed to be bad and insensitive. Bad boys get the girl, or so I noticed.

I remember being at my grandparent's house in the outer room on one darkened afternoon. I don't remember how many people were there, but I see them seated on old sofas and worn-out chairs with a spittoon in the middle of the floor. A clan gathering of sorts. I remember it was dark and cold. I can still see them spitting tobacco, quite some distance of several feet, sometimes missing...but with newspaper on the floor around the pot, it made clean-up not so much a mess. I am seated next to my grandfather, who for some reason is holding my hands in his. Perhaps wondering, *does this boy have what it takes to be the lead farmer?* I remember looking up at him as he looked over my hands and fingers. He observes out loud that my hands are too small and too delicate to be a farmer. I remember feeling lessened by that. Compared to his large and very calloused hands, like leather, if that be the measure of farmer, for sure what he says is true. What he did not know, nor did I then, that I was gifted with great hands with fine motor nerves in my fingers. Surgeon's hands.

Very handy for fixing mechanical things, which is so much a part of next generation farming.

My character and destiny were also shaped by my father's alcoholism, which he struggled to control. And he never really did—a dry drunk, as I think the condition is called, as he moved onto other addictions. I know now this is not a flaw of character weakness, but a condition needing treatment, which he got. But in my younger years, that never seemed to keep him sober. He'd be gone for a month at a time over those early years. Often between bouts, he was not able to get out of bed; I suspect deep depression, not well treated. I am prone to it as well. As oldest, I stepped in to fill his absence...my duty.

I do remember one summer, when I was fourteen, he was gone most of summer in rehab. It was a hard summer as his absence in the field was felt when all men needed to get the harvest in. A painful memory: the threshing machine was set up at our place as we were next on the list, but with neighbors, as well as his brothers and father, angry at Dad's absence, his father pulled the machine from us in the morning of threshing day. It was one of the very few times ever, out behind the garage chopping wood, cords, and cords for the coming winter, I cried. That afternoon, mother made her boys, the three of us, take two wagons and tractors up to Wilson's as he was next on list for threshing. We loaded sheaves from his fields onto our wagons and hauled them to our roaring threshing machine. The Cavanaughs owned the thresher when threshing was a farm community activity. Threshing was labor intensive. To pull Dad's weight was hard to do, but we did best we could. And we did eventually get our harvest in. The invention the "combine" did away with threshing machines. The Zen of change in action. Reverse the flow of threshing energy...bring the machine to the fields and everything about harvesting changed.

Upon Dad's return, I remember feeling a little strange and protective of my mother...an Oedipal moment! For sure in my childhood, I had my bad days, and sometimes many days in row. Some of them were frightening and painful. My life was completely farm centered. No time for after school activities. No time for dating. I missed a lot of "normal" psychosexual development, and that has been problematic. Kind of like Harlow's monkeys for not getting the right kind of contact at the right time, resulting in a harder time figuring out relationships. What I understand now is that we all got "shit" from our personal history to work through. The grist for the mill to mature. Manure is the stuff that makes things grow. I was raised in a violent environment; men and animals alike abused all around me. A sensitive boy, yet the oldest to pave the way. I learned to be violent to protect myself and my brothers and sisters from being bullied. I used to callous my knuckles by punching the barn walls. Touch my family, and they would answer to me.

I know that my strength to survive Vietnam came from my childhood, forged with the responsibility of being the oldest male in an Irish/French and Catholic farm family. And my path in life was something of a reaction to my Cavanaugh heritage as my mother as told me. Her bridesmaids had all offered condolences upon her marriage to Leo. "The Cavanaughs are hard living men, but they are great providers. Your children will never be hungry," they had told her.

My father was a lover and musician, not able to live up to the image of the hard man. I wonder if the alcohol and drugs gave him the courage. He ended up giving up on life and died, what I believe is, a premature death, mostly from a broken heart in early '70s. It was a slow suicide of dreams unmet and an inability to see the beauty that was around him, particularly in his beautiful wife. However, Leo did provide well, although sometimes in early years food was scarce, none of us ever went hungry. And setting up his wife to live in good comfort independently for the rest of her life surely was a measure of being a Cavanaugh. And I would guess from his perspective, his way of loving his beautiful "Tessie."

Without understanding the full meaning of my history, but now freed up from my parental destiny at age twenty-four, I was determined to follow my bliss. I thought of myself as toughened by my background and unafraid of hard work—it seemed as though Vietnam was pre-ordained.

I grew up thinking a real man, if I be any measure, would not be broken.

I now know better.

Harpers Ferry, June-July 1967

Harpers Ferry, West Virginia was the location of our in-country International Voluntary Services (IVS) orientation. In a beautiful, peaceful summer place, a group of recruits selected by IVS outbound for Vietnam assembled in preparation for cross-cultural training, Phase One. I was one of them, feeling special to have been selected.

I know now that I got a lot out of the pre-departure training; it was invaluable in whatever I did in Vietnam. While the specific learnings I have long forgotten, the general themes I remember. Get inside the culture to do your best work. Respect and enjoy the culture. Be of use in alleviating suffering through improved living standards. More food, better water, better practices for healthy living based on science.

My experience of that time was of slowly joining "normal" culture after four years of separation in Catholic seminary. From isolated and very shy Canadian farm boy to Catholic seminarian in the US, I did not have very much exposure to Americans qua "Americans." My, what an extroverted people, and most certainly daily contact with women my age was an all a new thing!

I came from the farm and minimal contact with girls my age. Other than the requirement of asking a girl to my high school prom, a test of manhood—and one platonic relationship—I was a virgin. The nuns pressured me to ask the unasked girl in my class to the prom. To please them, I did. I do not remember if I even kissed her good night. Or was I supposed to? I was terrified to be alone with an adult female. And I so very much wanted that not to be so.

For years I had been preparing myself for celibacy, which brought with it the relief of never having to confront the "first time" with a woman. By this time in my life, I was feeling very handicapped relative to my peers, and I did not want any girl to know how ignorant I was in the ways of sex. The assumption in the model of male sex development that I internalized is that men are supposed to know. And now here the women were in this free-form environment, bumping into me, some repeatedly so, even in my attempts to avoid them.

I recall most of my days at Harpers Ferry 1967 were filled with much discussion and interaction on cross-cultural adaption. I recall us being a group of about thirty or so in size, and I was among the group who would be agriculturalists. We were mixed gender, young, all white as I recall, college educated, volunteers, civilians, and all headed for Vietnam in a time of war. There was an instant sense of togetherness. I felt at home among people who, for whatever reason, were motivated to do this. We were all motivated to go to Vietnam and do good work, and we became a cohort group for support in that work. Later on, we would have some great times in Saigon, with heavy drinking and crazy dancing as a good way to blow off the stress…even during the most trying of times.

Still stinging a little from the "loner" label used to justify my dismissal from pursuit of priesthood, perhaps IVS's way seemed made for me. I wanted my new adventure to work. Still a farm boy at heart, I was now determined to see the world.

Our lifestyle in country would be equivalent to that of a Vietnamese schoolteacher. We were given a monthly stipend to live in the culture at that standard of living. (There were no ATMs.) Making a call across the globe was a big deal. I would learn that my Kon Tum home would be on the east side of city within a few blocks of the airport, which proved to be an interesting location. My assignment in Kon Tum did require me to travel frequently to Saigon, and by air only due to countryside security concerns. I was given the civilian equivalent of military "officer" privileges, which gave me access to military transportation and PX. Mostly though, I flew Air America. My willingness to use American support was part of a growing feeling of compromise that I would need to make if I wanted to go on. What I assessed as my pact with the devil to accomplish a greater good. Hardly any human endeavor of any great magnitude, big or small, is done without getting your feet dirty if history is any reference. The point is to not get sucked into the mud.

My general profile of that time at Harpers Ferry was of an observer. I spoke little. I joined in required activities, but in the free-form environment, my introverted nature and deeply ingrained shyness kept me to myself, which in many ways was adaptive. I was buying myself time to learn this culture's way of doing things. This is the first step in acculturation: observe. It just seemed odd to be practicing it in a culture that on the surface was very much like the one that I had been raised in, yet so different. A people so full of themselves.

In recruitment, IVS had offered me both positions to teach English in Algeria or work as an Agriculturalist in Vietnam. I never liked much being in front of a class, so I chose Vietnam and agriculture. Perhaps that choice was built into my emotional software from my background. I do wonder about the road not taken, though.

What may have been a part of my motivation to select Vietnam takes me deeply into personal issues having to do with a father who always "loved" the military. He regularly took us to Armed Forces Day at nearby Camp Borden, not far from our farms. And I did have nightmares as a child as the flashes and roar of nighttime training at the camp during the Korean War disturbed my sleep. Deeply frightened, I can still see the flashes on the walls of my bedroom and the images frightening me enough to call for my mother. As a young boy the noise of thunderstorms terrified me. Perhaps in reaction, I looked forward to Armed Forces Day. I so enjoyed walking around the machines of war, seeing the crispness of men in uniform. In Canada, at least in my home, there was a sense of deep respect for the military. We believed Canadians, disproportional to their numbers, suffered in fighting the Empire's wars. The Empire boys showed those English wimps how to fight!

I daydreamed as I milked cows and drove tractors of being in the Canadian infantry. I applied for Royal Military College at Kingston, Canada's West Point. I was offered Warrant Officer training. Second best. I deferred and chose Maryknoll. If I had been offered a position at Kingston, it is hard to believe I would have said no, and an entirely different life path to follow. How it was that I had both applications to priesthood and army at the same time is not an unusual story for upward-seeking young and Catholic men. And which, if offered, seems best?

So many junctures where my life could have been so different, and for this, the choices I made have felt "lead."

I was told that I would enter Vietnamese culture in civil war as an expatriate with each side backed by competing global social/political systems. We of that generation were raised with the threat of nuclear war. As we trained in school to protect ourselves, the threat felt so very real… this was the ambience of the time. Nuclear tensions were rising, and there was a sense it could end badly. It was only a lone intelligence officer on a Russian submarine stuck on the ocean floor who recommended to a Russian Captain, unsure of his orders given his situation, not to push the button that avoided nuclear holocaust in the matter of Cuba. The sense was that things were escalating in a high stakes game, and for the willingness of one side to back away from that madness, we owe a great deal to the peace movement. Imagine the alternative? The stew was in the pot, it just had to boil. I was part of that *weltanschauung*—world view.

I had been told by my IVS interviewer, as we met in a conference room in Boston's airport, that there would be "no war" where I was going in South Vietnam. The Highlands. I believed him. IVS was working with the Vietnamese Agricultural Ministry in Kon Tum, and a volunteer was spelling out and they needed a replacement. I was their choice. I would have access to the Bishop of Kon Tum and the Provincial Agricultural Chief. I had credence in both areas of power, which might give me the credibility to accomplish my mission. The specifics would come later.

My part in that drama was motivated by complexities of my history and the need to find a new way forward. I had given no serious thought to what I wanted next for myself in this life. There was no need. I had spent the first twenty years of my life preparing to run the family farms in Southern Ontario, Canada, and the next four preparing for a life-long calling with built-in support structures needed to focus on the work. Now with no option of going backward, I needed a vision. The felt sense was to get away, grow up, and gain perspective. If I had been born some years later when "native" vision quest practices were available, I suspect I would have done that! Or engage a shaman.

My vision quest was to go to Vietnam.

It turns out that whoever I am, I am an adventurer and explorer. Inner and outer worlds. I would later learn that it is part of my soul's nature to be a seeker of knowledge. Going as a western into another culture with the intention of teaching, educating, helping, and facilitating is an interesting story as we know. There are risks. Indeed, there is a general reaction against the need for missionary efforts, be they in the name of business, religion, or country, for these have wrought much harm upon the world but also much benefit. The world is richer for all the intermingling of foreigners. Let's just learn to do in more respectful ways!

The educational approach of IVS was humanitarian. In my mind, I was part of a mission that I experienced as Catholic social justice teachings without God at the center. My crisis of faith moved from atheistic to an agnostic mindset in matters of God. And God or not God, what does it matter, as long as the work of love gets done? If for example, I could grow rice that was stronger and healthier, and people came and asked me how to do this, I was there to respond. So much of what is "bad" about missionary efforts are grounded in a power to overcome the resistance to the message, and sadly, far too many times brutally so. IVS was "power with"—at least, that was the theory. I felt so very in sync with what IVS wanted me to do. A good farmer in a foreign land.

I would live in conditions of self-sufficiency in a lifestyle that, by American standards, would be well below poverty levels (no running water, no electricity), and I was charged with operating as if the war was not a major concern. I would learn to speak their language, listen to their music, eat, sleep, bathe, and work as a Canadian living in their culture. I was to act with respect for Vietnamese culture and people, and in a closeness of heart, I was to find a way to transmit and communicate. With the experience of mutuality, I would be able to work with and for the "locals"—a word that I always detested as demeaning. The hope was that what came of our efforts was of assistance, and in some ways, meeting the requirements of love. The word love was never used, but that was the sense of how I understood my mission.

At Harpers Ferry, I remember some grumbling about being an "international group" that was so decidedly "American" in outlook. Some in the group took a more radical, and what seemed at the time to me, a paranoid view of anything to do with the Establishment. There was suspicion, even fear, in the air. I would learn their paranoia was justified and sometimes miscued.

"Are you CIA?"

The words came from my left and rear in an afternoon training session at Harpers Ferry. I remember the room felt hot and sticky. I remember turning toward the sound in some state of shock as I realized the words were directed at me. I stuttered, as I still do when anxious, "No." And after some rather heated discussion about asking me to leave the group, the group accepted my response. We went on as though nothing had happened. The speaker was named Steve. He himself could have been a deep agent checking me out. I was Canadian. *Whose side was I on?* they could have wondered.

Steve was lean, tall, handsome, and highly intelligent. He had a great laugh and a warm smile. He was very verbal, and I was not. He had a strong personality, and by contrast I was a wallflower, a classic introvert. He was a city boy, New York Jew. I was a farm boy, Irish Catholic. Once we had a laugh about the incident, we bonded. We were drawn to one another, an experience of Eros—straight-guy-love asexual. We were drawn, but also never really understood one another. For him, the world was there for his experimentation. Rules were made to be broken. He was iconoclastic. Though at the time I was still quite agnostic, I prayed the rosary. I believed I could do good. On this, we agreed.

I do recall that the general bias of the information provided for instruction was pro-war. I do wonder if this bias might have been related to the fact that IVS success in Vietnam was highly dependent on the largess of the American military presence. The idealism of IVS began to hit the hard pavement of reality. I remember that tension peaked in intense meetings about the future of IVS in Vietnam in fall of '67 during language school in Nha Trang, South Vietnam. *Who pays the bills?* This is a primal juncture in much of human history. But that was all to come, after I continued training at Harpers Ferry.

I recall a sensuality about that time which both excited and alarmed me. I recall a beautiful afternoon, where I had some free time, walking across a dam on the nearby river. The dam surface was about 5 feet wide with maybe 3 inches of water running over my feet. Others were nearby. I had always cursed my shyness. I remember riding a bus to high school and a girl across the way hiked her skirt just above her knee to get my attention. I caught the motion out the corner of my eye but did not pay her any mind as I was so shy. I now see this trait as a gift that slowed me down. Made me look and listen. The sense of freedom, the feeling of the water on my feet, the sense of excitement as I carefully walked over the dam…I could not swim, and deep water lay just over the right edge.

What now strikes me as most odd about that time is how little the war was discussed as an issue that might have dramatic impact on us. It was as if everyone really believed that one could go into a nation at war and not be a part of it. Or they were not telling us. I sometimes wonder if we agreed not to talk too much about it, to not go to close to that topic, not to frighten us too much.

History shows that all war is barbaric, and there is something beyond barbaric when brother takes up against brother. Our band of IVS colleagues were entering a civil war at a time when each side was dramatically increasing the war effort in preparation for what each side saw as a fight to the death. For the Vietnamese, the war was personal: family; for the Americans, it was very impersonal: communism. Soldiers fight best when there is something personal at stake. The Vietnamese body count is a testament to this.

In this frame of mind, I began my first long plane ride from Washington, DC, US to Manila, Philippines.

Philippines, July 1967

Phase II of our IVS cross-cultural training was done at the University of the Philippines in Los Baños, Laguna, Philippines. The International Rice Research Institute was not too far away. The Institute was famous for what was being hailed as miracle rice—IR8. In later years, I would learn that IR8 did not live up to all its promise and created certain kinds of agricultural difficulties. Unforeseen effects are always a concern.

The trip to the Philippines took us from Washington, DC to Chicago and over Alaska with a stopover in Tokyo, refueling in Guam and then to Manila. The idea that this farm boy from Canada was going to fly halfway around the world filled me with a little anxiety and much excitement. There would be a 24-hour layover in Tokyo, which made Japan my first real taste of a different culture.

And taste it, I did. More than the crowded little cars buzzing along (or stopped dead in a massive traffic jam), my strongest memory of Tokyo is the horrific smell…air pollution gone mad. While I remember the bright lights of central Tokyo, I can still taste the eye-burning hotness of whatever it was that was on top of my choice of a traditional Japanese meal.

Three of us (Steve, me, and one other, whose name I do not remember) decided to break away from the group. We were going to see the "real" Tokyo. We were not interested in what we saw as tourist traps in gaudy, bright central Tokyo at night. We did not have to walk far from the bright lights to discover that the tone changed dramatically. It was quiet and mostly darkened shadows, narrow alleys with little lighting, the air filled with strange sounds and smells and sights. No one spoke English, nor did anything read in English. We ordered something to eat by pointing and gesticulating: fish and rice and something very red on top of it. I remember my first bite and the painful heat in my mouth, the burning and my eyes watering and the Japanese pointing and laughing at me. I could not tell if they were good-naturedly empathizing with my plight or enjoying an American in some real pain. I suppose both intentions could be true.

Such was the outcome of my first cross-cultural experience. Be careful what you eat.

The flight from Tokyo to Manila, the capital of the Philippines, was broken up by a stopover at Guam. A chance to stretch the legs. Standing at the top of the stairs of the Boeing 707 exit doors and looking out, I felt my first blast of real tropical heat. I remember saying to myself, *Wow, I've got to adjust to working in this stuff.*

By the time we arrived in Manila, we all felt weary. It was beginning to dawn on us that it was a big world, that we were a long way from home, and that the journey was just starting. We were whisked from Manila on buses, but not the kind I was used to. Unlike their American counterparts, these buses were Mercury built trucks in which the long flatbed had been converted to wooden benches. There was a canvas top supported by a bamboo framework with a single rail to prevent passengers from toppling overboard. These trucks were powered by smoky noisy Hercules diesels, which the driver seemed to delight in revving to a scream through each gear as we hurtled toward any oncoming obstacles. Like a game of chicken, it seemed. The roads were full of potholes and only by some unseen hand of divine guidance did we manage to avoid at the last moment head-on collisions. It was chaos on wheels.

Meanwhile, the passengers seemed quite unflummoxed by this style of driving. They carried with them boxed pigs, chickens, vegetables, and assorted goods, all bounced and jostled while a conductor made his way up, over, and around all of the people, things, and animals to gather tickets and collect money. I remember being amazed at his agility.

The University of the Philippines was a big adjustment. The classrooms looked modern enough, but the dormitory, as well as the lavatory and dining conditions, gave our first hint at the adjustments to come. The dorm consisted of long rows of double bunk beds; I was assigned a top bunk, and the dorm had so many windows it was like a large pole barn. The jungle sounds came directly to my ears. And strange sounds they were like some audio tape of jungle sounds, only this was the real thing. I remember being a little frightened at all the racket. It was hot and humid, even at night. The bed was open lattice wood, complete with two straw mats and a straw pillow. One mat was placed on the wooden bunk slats for a mattress and the other for a cover.

Even with that adjustment in sleeping habits, in addition to the heat, I do recall sleeping well. I took these to be a good sign that I might "make it" as some of my colleagues were already complaining about the "primitive" conditions. The bathrooms were a stretch as most of the toilets did not work—the only ones that worked were the infamous "hole in the floor." A practical solution, but not if you were not used to squatting, a challenge! Learning to do my business was my second cross-cultural adjustment... and one they forgot to mention in training.

The food was also strange to the taste. I remember being hungry, trying to find something that would both fill me and please the palate. This was not always possible. It was my first experience with the reality that hunger is as much psychological as physical. So many different smells... it's hard to remember, but some smelled good and a lot not so good. It seemed like nose training was next up in my cross-cultural training...the good news was that the nose adjusts that soon, what was so repugnant at first, faded into background.

The campus was quite lovely although not well maintained. Neglect and decay were everywhere although the professors and teachers seemed committed to their jobs. Each day I passed a tall statue of Magsaysay[5], a man who died for freedom, the engraving marking his heroic value.

---

[5] a former president of the Philippines.

We had long days and long hours of classes, road trips, and experiential learnings, which included learning to drive water buffalo. Several personal experiences shaped my development at this cross-cultural interface. I remember finding love in a rice paddy. I was planting rice, standing in water side by side with women all ages also planting rice. They were bent over, looking at each other, talking and laughing and planting. I remember wondering what they were saying about us as for every once in a while, some comment would strike them as hilarious. And then, one of the very young women came over to me, laughing at me for my inept planting of rice. She showed me. She then turned and smiled and said in halting but understandable English, "What is your name?"

"Jan. What is yours?"

"Marceline," she said. "Where are you from?"

"Canada." There was laughter in the background.

"Where are you going?" she asked. I told her Vietnam. Marceline frowned. "Do you have a wife?"

She giggled as I cleared my throat. "No." Now there was joyous laughter.

"I love you," she said. I think she really did, and maybe she would have made a great wife!

Another experience: to this day, I can still feel the knife at my throat. I can feel its edge on my artery.

Outside the university gates, in addition to any number of shops and services, was a grass-roofed bar where many of us volunteers gathered to share the day and enjoy a beer. And, oh my, was the San Miguel good. It was my first exposure to a higher alcohol content. I have never had beer that tasted so cold and so good since. Years later, I would occasionally have an imported San Miguel, but I never got the same pleasure.

Part of the pleasure was also the beauty and charm of the Philippine waitresses, with whom I had to be careful in making eye contact. Apparently, one of my very few and shy attempts to flirt communicated something very threatening. My intentions, while honorable, aroused an angry response from the waitress's boyfriend. I found that the Filipino male is very possessive and very fond of knives…and the next I knew, his knife was next to my throat. With due apologies, I was released. After that, I rarely looked at the foreign women. In the East, there is a subtle language of the eyes that is virtually unknown in the West.

That Filipino men friends walked around holding hands was a cross-cultural surprise. And taught a cross-cultural observer to hold no judgment. It just was. I saw that behavior a lot. Special Forces American holding in their laps Montagnard Special Forces on their way to battle. Known as fierce fighters.

Many of my male colleagues did not share my idea of respect for women to what, in my mind at the time, seemed to shocking degrees. For example, one evening, Steve (the one who challenged my CIA status) asked me to accompany him to another bar. We were buddies by now, so I agreed. However, Steve brought me to a brothel! I left quickly. I was trying to be accepting of my colleague's behavior, but deep in my mind and soul, I was totally appalled by this behavior. Not that I was not also a little curious, given that I was still a virgin, but I could not imagine myself behaving this way, even if my heart had not been given to another. I never did give in, except for a couple of incidents in the infamous "steam baths" of Saigon and Nha Trang, but perhaps more on that at another time. I am human, after all.

Steve was as shocked by my behavior (or lack of it) as I was his. Toward the end of our Philippines training, Steve asked if I wanted to go to Manila a day early before the rest of the group. "Go have some fun before Vietnam," he had said. We had permission to do this, so we went. I remember it was an awkward night on the town as a group of Filipinos, who Steve met, shepherded us from party to party, each one a little wilder than the *last*. I recall spending most of my time that night outside waiting. I rarely felt so out of place. The wild boy from Brooklyn and the shy farm boy made an interesting pair.

So naive at the time, I never thought twice about his choice to stay at the YMCA in Manila after our night out. Only now do I see that maybe Steve thought me queer and was trying to accommodate! I remember being alone in our room and hearing a knock at the door. A handsome young man, someone who we *had* befriended, came in and began making sexual advances toward me. I was shirtless because of the heat, and he claimed he liked my body hair and did not like my friend, who was relatively hairless. Just as I was about to ask him to leave, Steve entered, and my unwanted guest took his leave. After expressing my shock to Steve, who just laughed, he admitted that he had been approached by the same man with exactly the opposite "come-on" line. Steve seemed remarkably unflapped by all this, perhaps wondering what it was I was "into"…but we never had that conversation. I took my cues from him and just shrugged off the whole event.

I was learning from my wild Brooklyn friend that I was entering a world in which I would be exposed to so much. I would need to grow up quickly.

With this spirit, we rejoined the rest of the group, now in Manila, to continue our journey to Vietnam.

Saigon, August 1967

My first Vietnam memory is of passing through the arrival door at Saigon's Tan Son Nhut airport, full of people rushing around, and this Vietnamese male stepped into me and grabbed my arm.

I froze. I remember thinking him taller than most Vietnamese men and of lighter complexion. *From the north,* I thought. He looked me in the eyes while holding my arm firmly and intensely spoke these words in impeccable English: "Remember, a nation at war with itself is a nation of spies." I can still feel the release of my arm. And he walked away! If I tell my story true, that advice, more than anything, besides God's will, helped me survive. An angel perhaps!

My next memory is the drive from the airport, where I learned immediately that Vietnam was going to be even more different than I anticipated. Six of us, all male, jammed into a van with no seats, except for the driver and passenger side. The driver was a fellow in-country IVSer who, with great skill, maneuvered an old GM product to escort a group of us new arrivals to home base. I instinctively crouched behind him for some kind of protection from driving habits that made my experiences in the Philippines seem safe.

I remember seeing his finger pointing out a Vietnamese woman walking quickly in front us to avoid being hit. I instinctively followed his finger. First in

Vietnamese and then in English, he said to us, "Watching a Vietnam women's ass walk is like watching two little boys wrestle."

I never would have thought such a thing as I was too terrified to notice. The speaker spoke quite proudly of his observation, and with his midwestern accent, he glanced at us and clearly sought our approval. We all kind of froze…we did not cover that in cross-cultural training either! He seemed proud of his mastery of the language and his ability to drive in crazy traffic, the likes of which I have not experienced anywhere else in the world.

And then, the first few days in Vietnam are a blur of memories…I remember being at the volunteer agency's headquarters to meet and be greeted by leadership and in-country colleagues. I remember how crowded and hot and sweaty we all were. We were given some Vietnamese money for food and were approved for driving licenses as well. It was a busy time, but I remember thinking: *I am here. Smile.*

And a haunting memory: sitting at IVS headquarters in sweaty, brutal 90 degrees plus heat and humidity, crouched on the floor against the wall. I can still feel my body aching in that hot, crowded, and stuffy hallway with endless waiting to be processed for endless documents. I heard a roar in the distance and then a growing howl of engines hurtling at full throttle. Helicopters were just over the rooftops, shaking the buildings in their wake. This was my first and everlasting memory of the unique rhythmic *thwap, thwap* as its rotors pounded and snapped and grabbed the air—the sound of Huey helicopters passing over the compound. This first sound of war was to become indelibly imprinted in my soul. I would know this machine as my constant companion and reminder of the terrors of war.

It was my first body-shattering awakening to getting my war nerves: Welcome to Vietnam, the American War.

In journals, I wrote this about Saigon: "most certainly it is a vibrant, sprawling, dirty, hot, war-torn city." My mood, then, was shadowed by the dawning of an awareness: two years, which was the length of my commitment, seemed like a long time to live here.

Saigon was, and is, a very exotic sounding name for a city. The word feels good on the lips, foreign and sexy. Out of no disrespect to Ho Chi Minh, after whom the city is now named, I do hope someday the city is renamed as Saigon. I suppose that his name in history books forever is all that matters now.

Perhaps because I was overwhelmed with so much newness, I do not remember my first night in Saigon. I do remember that the group of us new volunteers were housed in a dormitory in a cooperative school, downtown from IVS. All of the men were in one large open dorm, the women in another. I have a powerful memory of the dreadful state of the bathroom areas. Most of the plumbing was broken with gushing water from broken valves everywhere. The showers worked intermittently; I remember one of my shower mates running out of his shower lathered with soap. He was mad as hell about the lack of water at that moment, cursing out loud about how he was supposed to get off the soap and get on with his day.

Culture shock was beginning to show itself. As part of stepping quickly into the culture, we were taught how to count money and how to order a breakfast in Vietnamese. While I don't remember my first night, I do remember my first morning, going across the street to get breakfast. It was my first exposure to Saigon traffic on foot. Like a river, the road traffic never stopped. So, to cross a busy street, pedestrians stepped into the traffic, eyes focused on oncoming traffic even as it came at them. Picking their way across traffic the mostly overburdened motorized and not bikes on two and three wheels with an occasional car veering around them as they navigated across the current. I observed and imitated what I saw. I had the tips of my shoe run over twice. *Next cross-cultural lesson: Take smaller steps.*

The bread and coffee we had for breakfast was my first exposure to French baking. The little hot baguettes buttered with jam tasted so wonderful. The French had left their imprint in many ways. This surprised me, given what I imagined would be a deep antipathy toward France and its legacy. Instead, I would learn that the French language and cuisine were widely accepted throughout Vietnam. Indeed, one could do business and find one's way around with the French while in Vietnam. Unfortunately, my French was limited to a barely passable academic knowledge of how to read and write it.

"Saigon days" is how I refer to any time I spent in the city. Of the city, I have images of broad avenues with beautiful homes and trees. And streets and sidewalks so crowded with the combination people in a mad rush on foot, on bicycles, tricycles, motorized and not, moving like water in a river with currents, eddies, cross currents, and whirlpools. One snaked one's way through, taking up any available space, looking for the tail of the snake in front of you so you could follow it. There were no rules, except do not hit anything. There were remarkably few accidents. As part of acculturation, in the first few days, I was granted a driver's license. I did drive there. Most would not.

Sometime in the first few days, my assignment to Kon Tum City in the Kon Tum province in the Central Highlands of Vietnam was confirmed. There were already two volunteers on site there: one male, who was being promoted and assigned to administrative duties in Saigon, and one female, a nurse who had several months left on her contract. I was replacing the male volunteer. I was charged with establishing a relationship with the Vietnamese Kon Tum Agricultural Director and to offer whatever support I could. I would go to Kon Tum within a few days and spend some weeks there getting myself established before going to Nha Trang, a city on the east coast of central Vietnam, for one month of intensive language study.

My journal notes indicate that shortly after learning all this, I felt disturbed and filled with anxiety about the uncertainty of future events. Apparently, leaving the comfort of the large group left me feeling a mixture of sadness and an ever-present aloneness. We had already been through a lot in a truly short period. I was about to be on my own in this very foreign environment, and even for this loner, it was a bit much.

As I moved from Saigon into the interior of the country, the extent of the depth and destructiveness of the war in Vietnam became more evident. Certainly, there *was* much evidence of a state of war in Saigon as well. All of the major buildings that were either of military or governmental importance were sandbagged and covered with barbed wire, with ever-present military guards, fingers close to trigger, and eyeing nervously with suspicion at any passersby. The city buzzed with the rumors of war, of impending attack, of dangers in the street. And attacks did happen. Foreigners were at risk for an ambush or were caught in local bombings. And even with attacks in the streets and danger of bombing, this did not stop us from traversing the streets and sidewalks, taking safety among the throngs of people.

After a while, the sense of danger in Saigon faded from awareness. Although, I was always, at some level, aware that any moment could be filled with bullets and shrapnel. I remember these thoughts clearly, even today, as I sat so long ago eating French ice cream in Pôle Nord before seeing more of the war for myself.

Reflections Based on Journal Notes, Summer and Fall '67

On approach during my first-time on-Air America to Kon Tum's one runway airport, I am looking out starboard side, and I see the bodies of planes from previous crashes off to the side.

After landing, there was no one around to greet me. I can still feel the blindness of the bright sun. What first struck me was the army Quonset huts. Mounds of sandbags and barbed wire were everywhere. That should have been my first clue. What I wonder now is why I never questioned going forward. I could have walked back onto the plane and left. I did not.

I can still remember stepping off that plane, a C-47, an old workhorse if there ever were such a thing among planes. I remember walking toward a square, white structure full of bullet holes...the terminal. There was no one there. After looking for a ride and finding no one around, I began to walk luggage in hand and tow to town. I still remember walking the sandy road, white hot in the midday sun. I walked no more than a partial kilometer before the sandy road slopped down across and up to the city of Kon Tum. I could see the buildings; it looked like center of town, all white and gray in the distance. There was a sharpness and purity about the hot air, so different from the sultry, wet air of Saigon.

I remember thinking as I was trudging along, *This is a long way from home.*

My journals from August 13, 1967 note that I had been in Kon Tum one week by that date, having been on the road almost two months, traveling from Canada, then two weeks in Harpers Ferry, then to the Philippines, and a couple of weeks in Saigon. I was culturally stressed out already, with radical changes in eating, sleeping, and living habits. "I am faced with some very complex problems in understanding my mission, as I face this complexity," I wrote. This complexity I referred to was the war. It was all around me.

By the 23rd of August, I note that Kon Tum "could be a real pain." On the 26th, I experienced my first "incoming" mortar and rocket attack. I still can feel the rise of nausea in my gut, as I was jarred from sleep, realizing their message was clear: "we are here, and we are coming to kill you."

"There would be no war" where I was going, as I was told by my IVS recruiter in Boston International Airport in April 1967. I can still feel the wry expression on my face, as I recalled those words several months later in the reality that I was facing. Perhaps what he told me, he believed as true, for I believed him, and perhaps by the time I arrived, the situation had deteriorated.

The Highlands of South Vietnam were an almost constant "red" zone in military "speak," the risk of attack always high. Now I understand as I watch Vietnam fall '67 and the Highlands in Ken Burns documentaries. All I knew at the time was how the war raged on around me. And oh, how it did.

Soon after my arrival, the Americans set up an artillery battery. Their largest cannon was just across the river to the south of Kon Tum off main highway. The blast of muzzle and the retort, even across town in my house, required me to steel my nerves against the ear splitting and body shuddering sound waves as they passed through me. At any time of day or night. In my memory, I can still hear those guns and their shells flying through the sky, sounding like boxcars slicing through the clouds. Their *whoosh, whoosh, whoosh* was a unique sound of war. I shuddered at the thoughts of the carnage wrought, as the echo of a shell exploding came back.

Kon Tum in a state of constant war readiness quickly shattered any illusions about there being "no war." There was war, and I was in it, like it or not. In Saigon, which was also a city subject to periodic attacks, the size of the city made the war feel less intense. Talking at breakfast about a rocket attack near the airport some 3 kilometers away was one thing, whereas in Kon Tum, the area was small, and the attacks felt personal. Each experience left me praying to God in the awareness that I might be next, and may it be quick. For me, Kon Tum was my own version of "hell in very small place[6]."

By September 6th, I wrote the following words:

War, where is Thy Gain?
Forests lying in ruin.
Animals, children screaming.
People moaning, staring.
Bombs slashing, cutting.
Bullets ripping, tearing.
Knives flashing, plunging.
War, where is Thy Gain?
Where is victory and
What is the Price?

I went to Vietnam with a philosophy of mission that could only be accomplished by my living among the Vietnamese. To do so, I would have to separate myself from association with any resources that might compromise my neutrality. I told any Vietnamese as soon as I could that I was a Canadian. Canada had played a positive role in keeping the peace after the French defeat. I felt that this might be to my advantage. Even my worn-out and open-top WWII army jeep painted yellow, and later my International Scout was subject of concern to me. I toyed with the idea of getting a motor bike to travel like the Vietnamese, but from the start, it was becoming clear to me that I would need a larger vehicle transportation for the agricultural work. How else was I to get supplies out to the center west of town? Part of my work involved hauling a lot of supplies…and part of that also meant hauling medical supplies into the refugee camps.

In war, all resources go to victory, or surely, the enemy will be victorious.

---

[6] As noted in *Hell in A Very Small Place* by Bernard Fall.

My efforts to define and stick with my mission brought me into conflict with both civil and military alike in Kon Tum. This was not what I had bargained for. I was young, and I did not yet know that life gives you exactly what you need on whatever journey you portend. The lesson was often not clear at the time. The Americans wanted me to live with them in their compound and be part of their "hearts and minds" mission. I wanted to strike out on my own. Efforts to strike out on my own consisted living in the house that IVS rented for its Kon Tum volunteers.

The home consisted of a large living room area and two bedrooms on either side. To the left toward the back of that great room sat a door to the kitchen with a charcoal stove and no running water. The toilet mostly was an infamous hole in the floor. To the left of the toilet area, in back of kitchen, was an unfinished room…and in time, a bomb shelter.

The front of the house had a little garden area, between the porch and the road, and around the left side was the well pump for water and a place for storage of charcoal—my source of fuel for fire. All water was boiled and doctored with little white pills to prevent malaria. Some of my colleagues suffered misery beyond misery with bowel ailments from water containing pathogens toxic to the American gut.

Light came from kerosene lamps. The ceiling over the living room area was vaulted with exposed beams and whitewashed plaster, giving the room an airy, French feel. There was no glass in the windows, only bars. When I bathed—standing baths at water bowl—children would come to the windows and point, laugh, and giggle at the foreigner.

I bought food at the local market to make my own breakfasts, but I entered a meal contract with a local restaurant for dinner and supper. Every day, there was a siesta from noon till around 2:30 p.m. The Vietnamese diet was strange in taste to me, particularly their fondness of *Nuớc Mắm*, roughly translated to mean dead fish water. It was prepared, as I understand, by collecting the water that comes from decaying fish. Like most things, if one stays open (the smell and taste is odious to the Western nose at first), you adjust. I did come to love *Nuớc Mắm* and the many kinds of rice dishes. To me, it seemed to be a healthy diet.

Even my choice of an eating plan was a source of annoyance to my fellow Americans, who took my choice to mean a rejection of them. In time, when my mission became less Vietnamese focused, I did eat more frequently at the civilian and military compounds. Sometimes, we were ordered to stay in the US Military Assistance Command, Vietnam (MACV) compound for the night when the threat level was High Red. I needed to make compromises to make for a better working environment.

There were many kinds of civilian contractors in Vietnam. Most of the civilians lived on prefab-compounds with enclosed yards and barbed wire on perimeter. In one corner of the property, a diesel-fired generator created the electricity to run pumps for running water and air conditioning. Each man had his own room, with a common kitchen area large enough to seat everyone. I would occasionally go there, both for purposes of contact with people who could influence some of my work but also get a shower. I knew when one of the men offered to let me use the group's shower room that I had torn down some of my fences.

Meals were held in a common area, prepared by Vietnamese women who also cleaned and did laundry. In some compounds, some of the "maids" would provide sexual services. In one infamous compound on a coast near the sea, women were available for a special kind of "alarm clock" services...if one was interested. I was always somewhat drawn to that, but I never had either the courage to ask or the lapse in moral judgment to partake. In the culture I was raised in, such things were not done. I did entertain fantasies of what that might be like. Most of the men were confused by my not doing so...thought me "queer." Many began to call me "monk"—and that moniker was closer to the truth than I knew at the time.

The American food, most of which was processed, frozen, or dried, was obtained on food runs in small, armed convoys to Post Exchange in Pleiku. To get supplies for myself I would join them, me and my M3 riding shot gun. When combined with local foods, the taste was interesting. Some of it was great, but sometimes, what was very "American" looking tasted quite different.

Kon Tum, August 1967

For administration purposes, South Vietnam was divided into four corps. Kon Tum City was the capital of Kon Tum province in what is referred to as the "Highlands" and part of what the Americans referred to as II Corps. The western edge of the province bordered Laos and just inside that was the infamous "Ho Chi Minh Trail."

Travel in and out of Kon Tum was both safer and more efficient by plane. Surface transportation was unreliable, the roads were often mined, and certainly, any vehicles were subject to search by the Viet Cong. I learned quickly that the countryside, at least much of it, was under the strong influence of what to the American military was the enemy. Since the South Vietnamese and their American counterparts did not control the roads, the Americans had set up their own air transportation for both servicemen and civilians. On most of my many trips between Saigon and Kon Tum, I flew Air America. When I was responsible for larger freight, I used military transport. To facilitate that mode of transport, I was given a government rating that gave me "officer" privileges. This rank not only made my movement between these cities possible, but it also gave me a priority status, although not a very substantial one. I often was given the message that as a civilian, I was little better than third-class mail. As long as they got me there, who cared.

I remember my first flights on Air America because of the contrast between the style and comfort of their vintage WWII C-47 cargo planes and Pan Am's 707 that brought me over. C-47 seats along each side of the aircraft were canvas and iron frames attached to a visible airframe. Passengers sat side by side, each seated directly across from each other. When ready for takeoff, I could hear the rear loading door slam shut and locked. Then the engines coughed and sputtered to life with a roar that was not dampened much by the aluminum skin so thin. I can still see it vibrating in the airframe, hoping the rivets would hold under the strain of takeoff. There were no cabin doors, so passengers could observe the pilots. I would always watch on takeoff, copilot holding the throttles in full position, his head turning slowly left to right, his eyes scanning the instruments for any signs of distress. What a vibration and roar. The pilot holding her steady as speed increased, this plane awkward on the ground, but looking straight ahead, eyes just above the horizon. At V1, the pilot would have his hands already locked on wheel, ready to pull the stick back as the copilot called out V2. At lift off speed, I could feel the strain on the airframe as the engines groaned and pounded in protest, the weight of the always fully loaded (and maybe a little more) aircraft weight.

Once airborne, the flight engineer, always a Vietnam male dressed in military garb, would leave his post at the rear of the aircraft, carefully keeping his balance as he walked, leaning forward as the newly airborne plane pitched and rolled. His mission was to peer out at the engines, first starboard then port. Check…no leaks, no smoke, no fire. On several occasions, what he saw caused him to scurry forward to the pilots, who would quickly begin emergency landing procedures. Once on the ground, flight mechanics would run around and tighten a few bolts, retighten oil, and fuel caps. Give the tires a kick. Then, one of them would give the signal to pilot to fire up. Peering out, I could see the exhaust pipes of the big engine popping smoke and snapping fire like a dragon as the starter pushed pistons to compression and partial ignition. Just as I wondered if this baby was going to start, I'd see huge puffs of black smoke, then full ignition and a mighty roar. Then we'd taxi to the base of the runway, with brakes locked for "run up" before takeoff, until engines burned hot and clean, and then in a lurch as the brakes released. Off we would go again on a wing and a prayer.

Air America's Saigon to Kon Tum flight was never direct. The fight path went from Saigon to Nha Trang, then sometimes up to Qui Nhơn, then to Pleiku, and then to Kon Tum. Four take offs. If we left early morning, we'd be in Kon Tum by noon. In the rainy season, the fog over the Central Highland was so heavy that we would be buffeted about in the clouds and fog-shrouded mountains for what seemed like forever, expecting at any moment to collide with a mountain. It was during these flights that I came to deeply respect the skill of the mostly old, balding, white pilots and their aged planes. The rough air of these flights, combined with fear, caused many of the passengers, particularly the Vietnamese, to become sick. Hence the nickname for the Nha Trang to Kon Tum portion of the flight: "The Vomit Comet."

From the beginning of my stay in Kon Tum, every day was periodically punctuated by machine gun and rifle fire. At night, the sounds came from all directions with frightening intensity. I was totally unprepared for the sound of war. Occasionally, there would be a quiet night, which was both unnerving and a blessing.

All that fall, there was war tension in the air. I remember one time, in the Officers Mess in MACV, over drinks officers heralded the coming of a "real fight." One could feel this tension as a denseness in the air. It is a feeling like no other, a sense of death with every breath. There were many signs of it coming, like the gathering of ferocious storm.

I vividly recall visiting the MACV after a particularly noisy and terrifying night and seeing my first evidence of a rocket attack. The screeching sounds themselves were terrifying, but to have the sound and fury of war wake me from deep sleep, often alcohol-induced, in an instance, again and again and again, is hard to forget. Visitors from Saigon, another city under siege, left Kon Tum "shaking" even after only a 24-hour visit as I helped them on the plane. They had no real war nerves. The sounds of war were a fearsome thing. To survive as anyone who lived during that time did, you armored up: got your "war nerves." You steeled your body and soul from sound and fury of war.

Standing in the MACV compound one morning to get my Army Post Office delivered mail, I could hear, and imagine even today, José, an American civilian nervously laughing as he pointed at his shrapnel-shattered International Scout. Amid an American military compound, their message was clear: "We are here, and we are coming to kill you."

War is at once very impersonal and very personal.

Ford Broncos and International Scouts were the most favored vehicles for American government workers in the outposts of Vietnam. It was a common rumor that the CIA used black Broncos, which I thought odd—trying to hide in plain sight but not well enough, I thought.

Daily living needs were purchased from the military PX at Pleiku, some 70 kilometers south of Kon Tum. I was offered a bedroom at this compound. Frankly, since I was already lonely for American style food, a hot shower, and comradeship, this option was very appealing. There was also a level of fear in the appeal. The American mentality was that life outside the American compound was dangerous. In their experience, the Viet Cong were everywhere because the entity with which they fought was mainly invisible. The American civilians socialized with the military officers headquartered at the MACV compound. Boozed-fired stories were told of friends dying, of Viet Cong attacks, of mined roads, and most persistently, rumors and rumors of impending attack.

Everyone was afraid all the time. I was beginning to absorb the fear made more real by the sounds of war. On August 26, mortar rounds were fired into town, seemingly to disrupt the provincial elections. These rounds seemed to be an attempt to warn the Vietnamese sympathetic to the South to snub the "elections," which to the Viet Cong were bogus. It was sort of their way of saying, "We are here, and we are very close." The message was not without effect; people died that night.

The choice to live at the IVS house instead of the compound was not without its complications. The female IVS volunteer still lived there. She would be leaving in January of 1968. I was to be in Nha Trang at language school for all of September anyway, so rather than finding a separate location for me, we agreed to share the house since finding a new location was not easy. Given the house's relatively large size and separate bedrooms, we agreed that it could accommodate us both until her departure. Besides, her work at the Catholic-run hospital of Minh Qui on the outskirts of Kon Tum often required her to be gone for days at a time. I felt sort of okay with the arrangement, but knowing my heart felt connected to Luisa, by puritan Roman Catholic standards, I was living with another woman. But I really felt okay with this—I even kind of liked the idea.

As part of the settling in, I met with the Vietnamese director of agriculture for Kon Tum province. He spoke reasonably good English with a French accent. He was a stately, thin, old man with exceedingly long chin whiskers, and a 3-inch fingernail on the small finger of his left hand. I knew these were signs of his status. He was a kind, still man, so much the picture of a wise old Eastern man. My meeting with him clarified my growing sense that the war effort was primary. Basically, he had no money to support programs and no money to hire people, which meant that the training center was not in service. It had no manager; it had no program; it was in a dangerous area outside Kon Tum to the west; it had no students. The potential students were all off to war. I could work with the Montagnard, the native peoples in the Central Highlands of Vietnam. He would identify someone from the Bahnar tribe to be my contact. At least this was something to get me started. The job description felt within the broad outlines of my organization's intent for my mission. To work almost exclusively with the "tribal populations" certainly seemed worthwhile, and it appealed to my support "for the outsider" instinct. I could never tell whether I was assigned this because of an intent to downgrade my mission by having me work with a socially outcast group, or whether the intent was an attempt on the director's part to respond to a justified need. Regardless, did it matter?

Within a few days, I met my Montagnard counterpart. He was a man in his mid-twenties, a schoolteacher who spoke excellent English. He was eager to have my attention, and he had an agenda: visit the training center, which in his view, was not so dangerous a place to grow food for displaced villagers. But first, I had to go to his village to discuss plans. His manner was easygoing and relaxed, and he seemed to be always smiling, even when I came to know he had other feelings. His name was Jhar as I recall.

I had been shown the training center within days of my arrival in Kon Tum by the volunteer who I was replacing. He was a large bodied Hawaii-American nicknamed "N." He was always helpful and friendly. He left shortly after my arrival to assume his responsibilities in Saigon. Once again, I was left feeling like a bird tossed out of my cage, wishing for more time with him. Life gives what it gives; learn the lesson. In the hand off to me, N did give me a connection with the Vietnamese government, without which I would have been lost. He did his part in the handoff: my entry point.

I drove Jhar in my sputtering International Scout, which was shades of brownish yellow to give a sense of neutrality…I thought. I remember this because I carried the belief that this distinguished me from the typical coloring of American vehicles, both military and civilian, making the Viet Cong less likely to attack. Of course, the North Vietnamese Army not knowing me was another matter as well. And probably none of it was true…just helped me get through.

The training center was several kilometers to the west of Kon Tum. The one notable feature along the drive was a cemetery. I always felt mildly anxious driving by this graveyard. Something about the way locals buried their dead above ground gave me the chills. I came to see this as just another way to re-assimilate our bodies back to dust. The center itself consisted of 2 hectares of land (roughly 5 acres), and a small-thatched roof building. The building was in a state of disrepair, the land overgrown with weeds. There was a small plot near the building, which was planted with smaller plots for growing plants. Why these were being grown and by whom was never made clear to me. I always suspected it was someone's private vegetable patch.

Walking around the center, I made notes on what Jhar thought would help his people. Afterward, we headed to Jhar's village, which as I recall was to the north and east, not even a kilometer or so outside Kon Tum. While the main roads and streets within Kon Tum were smooth flat sandy surfaces, dusty in dry season and muddy in wet, the roads outside Kon Tum, whether secondary or primary, were full of huge potholes with the sandy surface turning quickly to mud when wet. The roads were in fact much more suited for motorized bicycles as it was easier for them to dodge the bad spots. We bounced our way back into Kon Tum then out beyond the airport. After a kilometer or so, the main road turned into not much more than a footpath. We walked the last few hundred meters into a clearing, which when I stepped into it, felt like I was going back several thousand years in time. This was Jhar's village.

I had heard of the Montagnard tribes in my cross-cultural training, and once again, I had the experience of "nothing prepared me" for what I beheld. I focused first on the houses. They were made of wood and thatched leaves and stood on posts, at least 6 to 8 feet off the ground. Entrance to each house was by means of a pole with notched steps. Seeing the expression on my face, Jhar explained, as he escorted me to his home, that this type of house protected his people from wild animals and kept them off the dampness of the jungle floor. *A very practical solution to the interface between man and nature*, I mused to myself.

After gingerly climbing up into his home, one of the larger ones in the village, the afternoon was spent talking and drinking tea. In later weeks, we would make plans, but that afternoon was spent doing what the Bahnar do well - enjoying being alive. He introduced me to friends and the village elders, and after much talk, the rice wine was brought out: a sign that friendship was being extended. Only the men were present. Rice wine is extremely potent with a very bitter, pungent taste. Made in tall earthen jars and all sipped from the same straw. It is sake times ten it seemed, in bitterness of taste and potency. That afternoon was the first of many afternoons when I certainly was "over-the-limit" as me and trusty Scout meandered back to town.

Kon Tum was situated on the river valley of Đắk Bla. Tall hills and old mountains similar to the Catskills of New York surrounded the valley. Located on the north/south axis was a main highway that ran up the western side of city. Leaving Kon Tum to go south required crossing a heavily guarded bridge that crossed the river. The civilian American compound that I was invited to be part of was on the northeast bank of the river within a hundred yards of the bridge. My IVS house was situated on the east side of the downtown area within a few blocks of airport. From that location, the noise of military air transport was ever present. As very few people had cars, the downtown area was not busy in that sense, but the combination of bicycles, motor bikes, ox-drawn carts, and old buses could produce a lot of noise and dust. I do remember being in my first traffic jam at the main intersection—two ox carts, an American personnel carrier, my Scout, and a poorly parked bus. It was the ox carts that caused a wry smile as I thought about how different my life had become.

I remember that August, my housemate Joan invited me to accompany her to a party that was being given to honor a departing guest. I would know him as Lou, a physician who came to Vietnam over the summer to assist Dr. Smith. It was time to say goodbye to him. Lou was a GYN surgeon who was training to be a Jungian psychoanalyst while preparing for ordination as a Jesuit priest. He was a unique and a gifted man. He would come over the following summer as well. We eventually became great friends as his interests and values were more in line with mine. He asked me to assist at surgeries… my first, a prolapsed uterus.

I do not remember much about the party, except getting there. The getting there had to do with my deciding to ride with Joan on her motor scooter. My trusty Scout was getting a new clutch and not available. She asked if I wanted to drive it, I suppose out of deference to our ingrained male/female roles. And rather than being direct about the fact that I had never driven, let alone driven and carried a passenger on such a vehicle, I accepted her offer. It was as if I was saying to me, to her, to the world, I can't go to the party driven by a girl on a motor scooter. I remembered struggling to get us going upright and straight. And I did. We laughed and bonded as friends over my audaciousness. She was a brave woman!

The guest list included all the senior American leadership, civilian and military. I was introduced to them all. I felt strange about this, given my growing antiwar feeling.

My weeks in Kon Tum before language study had been successful to some degree. I had met an interesting cast of characters. I had staked out my identity such that when I returned from language study, I could focus on my mission and developing my job description. I was here to help the Montagnard. I could write my monthly report to Saigon with some confidence that I had found a purpose for being in Kon Tum.

Nha Trang Language Study, September 1967

Nha Trang is situated on the South China Sea on the east coast of South Vietnam. Near the city was a huge American air base, Cam Ranh Bay. I remember driving around on it, so large in size, I felt I was back stateside. There were paved and lighted streets, well-built housing, running water, electricity, and most of the amenities of American life in a well-stocked PX.

The IVS house in Nha Trang was near the city's airport, and the racket day and night is ingrained in my memory. At sunrise particularly, the whine and roar of airplane engines bombarded my ears to awaken me. I can still hear in memory the roar in "run up" to test the engines before takeoff.

The house was a lovely old home: large, airy, and comfortable. But it was not large enough to house all the language students. I recall there were about eight of us. It was decided I would stay with Don, a newbie, like myself, who was assigned to Nha Trang. He had space in his place for a bed cot.

I suppose we were a good match as we respected each other…though we were also quite different.

Don lived with a Vietnamese family on the outskirts of the city in one large room (half the house), and the Vietnamese family lived in the other half. They provided meals as part of the deal. Don was a tall, blue-eyed, blond-haired man who was very committed to the principles of IVS. Conservative white and male, he was a man deeply embedded in Christian fundamentalism. A well-intentioned lost soul, I think is how he saw me. I was agnostic about almost everything and becoming more so every day—how could a God of Love allow such a mess? With this as the question, we had many intense and enjoyable discussions about war, politics, religion, and the state of the world. This was back in the day when one could have such heated debates and at the end, shake hands and have a beer, maybe each of us a little wiser. He drove like a maniac, whizzing along in his gray Land Rover, seemingly oblivious to how close he came to bumping, knocking over, and running over the Vietnamese bicyclists and pedestrians. It seemed to me he almost enjoyed scaring them—he for sure scared me—as we made our daily trips to and from language study. I often thought it was only the hand of God on the steering wheel that got us safely back and forth.

Two strong memories emerge from living at his place: the Vietnamese music and the beach. The family played Vietnamese music, very loudly, throughout the day. I remember the sound screeched on my nerves. The beach was a short walk from the house. I used to go there at sunrise and watch the sun's rays fill the beautiful bay. Sometimes I would stand facing east, the sun just about to break the night, my arms stretched open to let the first beams of sun penetrate my heart: imagining Luisa. From Luisa's letters, I knew she and friends had rented a beach house on Cape Cod. Facing end of summer fun and getting ready to go back to college, she seemed nervous and unhappy. The depth and frequency of our correspondence was a measure of our desire to keep our relationship alive and growing.

Both ends of the beach were covered with barbed wire, but other than this evidence of war, I always felt safe, warm, and filled with good spirits as I sat in the early morning stillness. The calm before. With the morning sun, the sounds of war would arise again.

On September 10, 1967, we began our studies with Mr. Q, a gray-haired man with a kind smile. He was a Catholic refugee from Hanoi. He was a good and patient teacher who interjected stories of his life in Hanoi, which he clearly missed. He spoke of the beautiful parks and of the beauty of North Vietnamese women. He had a soft voice full of life; it filled me with respect for whatever his subject.

The Vietnamese language, with its six tones, was difficult for me. Perhaps too dense of mind, or perhaps from too much time with the din of engine pistons beating on eardrums, it was difficult for me to distinguish the tones, to hear the nuance, and make the subtle change in my vocal cords needed to make the sound. A word could mean yellow, love, or feces, depending on the tone. I worked hard at it, though my work in the Highlands with the Montagnard would dilute my efforts to become more fluent as I would eventually focus on the local dialect. The overall result was that I never developed the high level of language proficiency that had been one of my goals for life in Vietnam. To this day, I am disappointed about that reality.

Language study was in the morning and afternoon, seven hours a day for four weeks, as I remember. My journals reflect that midway through language study that my mood was somber. I am missing the United States more than I know. For example, after one beautiful afternoon on the beach, we visited a USO. I walked in, smelled hamburgers and french fries cooking, heard a song by the Mamas and the Papas, and found myself filling up with tears. Gustatorily and auditorily, I was confronted with how much I missed American burgers, as well as Luisa. They were playing one of our songs.

My journal of that time reflects a restless and confused mind. On October 23, I wrote that I had a "sometimes restless empty feeling" with IVS, and "how it is to position itself vis a vis the war." The idealism of IVS and the realities on the ground in war hit the proverbial shit-fan. I remember the meetings, where the idealists and the realists battled it out. I do not remember the specifics but remember that things were resolved such that I would be going back to Kon Tum, siding with the realists…making the best of a difficult situation.

Kon Tum, Winds of War, October-November 1967

The seriousness of the war came to me in stages. The din of the Huey gunships on my arrival in Saigon, the rumors of war, the sandbags, the barbed wire, soldiers everywhere, and the necessity of Air America, given the precarious security in the countryside. I was confronted more and more personally with the reality that Vietnam consisted of armed camps everywhere. The cities were isolated because the enemy controlled much, if not most, of the land and water in between. With each stage, the reality of war became more personal.

So, when I returned to Kon Tum in late October from language study, I met Col. C (Commanding Officer Military Assistance Command Vietnam, MACV) to brief me on Kon Tum's security situation. According to Col. C, in my absence from Kon Tum, the war had grown more serious. Only now, watching Ken Burn's series on the Vietnam War, do I realize the full meaning of what he said. A great push of war came through the Highlands in fall '67, and only after watching the documentary did I comprehended the enormity of why I experienced what I did that fall.

As he showed me charts, Col. C noted that the Viet Cong were active in the surrounding villages with the activity increasing. In addition, North Vietnamese Army (NVA) regulars were diverting off the Ho Chi Minh Trail just to the west of Kon Tum. The colonel had already lost two men killed by road landmines. One of them I had briefly met. He had been killed on a road that I planned to travel later that day. I wondered my fate if he had not gone first and died. All of this news was disturbing; the possibility of death by a landmine was unnerving. I was thunderstruck. His briefing was consistent with my perceptions. The sights and sounds of war bombarded me. Particularly formidable was the sporadic blast from the huge guns of the recently installed American artillery battery just across the river. In my house, which was nearly a kilometer away, if the wind was in the right direction, the roar of the muzzle blast sent shock waves painful to the ear and vibrating to the body. I would always wonder, *did someone just die, or is someone screaming in pain, wishing for death? Was that someone just a bystander in this terrible conflict?* In war, there are only two sides; yet here I was defining a third side, a side of neutrality. How strange I must seem to both American and Vietnamese alike.

Col. C felt responsible for my safety. I never believed that his intentions in briefing me were manipulative. He was a big man: white haired, reddish-white complexion, and came across as good hearted. Whatever his private reservations about the war and chances of victory, he seemed genuinely committed to the American cause.

Despite his cautions, and despite my nervousness, I decided to proceed with my mission supporting the tribal peoples. I had the support of the bishop. *Mines are rare*, I thought. My mission to the tribal peoples was clear, and they would protect me. I would be careful. I remembered the advice of that Vietnamese man at the airport as I entered Vietnam: eyes were everywhere to help me see. I started my residence in the IVS house and began eating downtown as a chance to practice talking Vietnamese with locals. I started a routine of visiting the Montagnard villages to learn how I might be of assistance, particularly to the refugees. I would be a known entity. These visits were always with Jhar as a guide, liaison, and translator. On some days, on Jhar's advice, we changed our village visit plans. We also made periodic visits to the training center to attend to the garden of vegetables…perhaps there were no students for classes, but we could still use the space to grow food. And we did.

The Central Mountainous region of South Vietnam was different from my previous geographical experiences. In Southern Ontario, the geography consisted of huge fertile farm valleys surrounded by forested hills. The climate was continental. Very cold, long winters with relatively brief, and sometimes, hot summers were separated by a long, cold spring, and a brief but beautiful fall. My training in the Philippines was geared toward flat wetland rice farming.

Kon Tum did have arable land. It seemed much of it was owned by rubber plantations. The Montagnard lived in small villages and sustained a lifestyle thousands of years in the making, living off the land according to their needs, respecting the laws of nature. We could learn from them in regard to how live in harmony with nature. The war was changing all that as they were forced for safety's sake to seek refuge closer to Kon Tum. The American military strategy was a version of "make my day." If they couldn't control the countryside, they would make the countryside into "free-fire zones." If it moved, you killed it… Vietnam was a dirty war. To house the growing refugee population, numerous new villages were constructed using more modern building materials, like squared sawed wood and sheet metal for roofs. The habitat was nothing like the forest the refugees once knew. These villages existed on razed lands, and the forest cut far back for security purposes. The inhabitants needed help…how to feed them now that the traditional food sources were gone? This was the beginning of Kon Tum's refugee problem. The words "war" and "refugee" are as one in my mind, and even more so today, as we see the horrors of war visited on our brothers and sisters on global networks.

My sojourns into the villages included these new villages as well as the older ones. Whether new or old, what was so evident was the natural friendliness, warmth, even innocence of these mountain people. I remember being in one of the villages and having a conversation about the word "ocean." The native speaker had no word for that…I can see him trying to imagine. We came up with "water after water with no end." I have no idea what prompted that conversation, but I remembered it was important to connect with him. As I became a more accepted presence, their natural shyness (perhaps wariness) for the foreigner diminished. I was invited to attend and be present for the celebratory rhythms of their life. I remember being very drawn to them. I was searching for something different, and their nature oriented, even-tempered, earthy, simple lifestyle appealed to me—as well as their very graphic language and laughter as they went about daily activities.

I must have been indicating in many ways my interest, as I recall, after another afternoon of sipping too much rice wine. The village leader offered me one of his daughters in marriage. The message was clear: come join us, be one of us. I still remember her dark eyes smiling, radiant, her youthful and bare-breasted body glistening in the humidity of the rainy season. Even with much protestation to accept, I said no. And I was set back a little, I think, in gaining their trust. For sure, marriage would have put me in the middle of their culture…to be of service. I often wonder now, in my old age, what might've been. I did not take that path because my intentions would be unclear: to take a Montagnard bride when I was unclear of my intentions with her would violate my sense of appropriate behavior. I was here to help. Besides, my heart was still feeling the pull toward Luisa, who was far, far across the "water after water with no end."

In my journals, I noted that I felt pleased with my progress in Kon Tum. However, in the days and weeks of late October and early November, the rumblings of war grew closer and louder. Jhar, my Montagnard guide, teacher, and friend, who was extremely helpful in my obtaining quick entry into their culture, was warning me of this. On the days we could not go into a village, the Viet Cong would be there doing their own "winning the hearts and minds" programs. This reality was never openly stated; I inferred it from Jhar's comments about the nearness of the Viet Cong. He was Catholic. It was through the Church that he had received his education. He was afraid of the Viet Cong, as he believed, that if they won, they would be vehemently anti-Catholic and would kill him and his family. It was as if he had put his faith in this foreign religion, which brought him into conflict with anti-foreign forces. I could sense his fear, but this never stopped him from doing what needed to be done.

One issue emerged very quickly: the poverty. The older villages around Kon Tum were in better economic condition because these villages did have communal land, which was used to grow food. These foods, combined with the legendary hunting prowess of these people, provided their diet. With hunting territory limited by war, particularly in the newer villages, how to feed all the people was a big part of my job. Jhar and I hit on the idea of growing cash crop mushrooms. There was a market; all we needed to do was get the crop growing, make some money, and get others do to the same to become a more self-sufficient community. I knew a little about mushroom growing; harvesting mushrooms was touched upon while we were at the University of the Philippines. But Jhar knew more. Jhar knew of village rice straw piles deep inside the forest that could be used to grow them. And to get there, we needed to cross the raging Đắk Bla river. I remember that afternoon of mushroom planting very vividly.

I remember standing in the middle of the village and looking around. The strangeness of the village setting was still new to my eyes. In this very strange view, I felt frozen in time, not sure what next to do. Then I saw him coming down the path: Jhar proudly marching through his village, spores in hands, holding them like a priest leading a procession as this parade of men, women, and children joined in the march down to the river. I joined in. The river, Đăk Bla, was flowing very rapidly due to the rainy season and was about 50 meters across at that point. Not too wide in distance, but it still seemed dangerous as I saw the muddy waters running fast. Even strong swimmers would struggle. I heard a shout and saw Jhar and others dragging a dugout canoe. "It's over there," he said, pointing across the river, probably seeing the quizzical look on my face.

I don't swim, I thought to myself. I imagined drowning in what, by this time, seemed like an angry river with rapids just waiting to swallow me up.

"We may get wet," he said. *No shit*, I thought as he stripped down to his loincloth. I striped to my white briefs. I remember standing there on rivers edge as the whole village of children and women were laughing and running at me, cheering on the foreigner. The women and children touched my body all over, my white body so out of place...and their astonishment that I had body hair.

We made it across. I can still see the muddy water rushing so fast near the top of the very narrow canoe. Next, I remember walking some distance and finding bales of straw constructed to plant the mushroom spores. What I did not know then, although for sure hinted in the winds of war, is that events would outrun seeing that harvest.

Bahnar people in their natural habitat did not wear much clothing but adjusted their ancient practices to adapt to Western sensibilities. At the time I was there, the men wore a loin cloth as well as a cape in the cooler season. The women wore a square piece of cloth fastened and wrapped around their waist. It was ankle length, very modest, but with thigh-high slits. Bare breasted. Upon going into town to market, in deference to Vietnamese sensitivities, they covered their breasts. To this day, I do not understand the fear of female breasts in public view, the power of breasts hidden.

The naturalness of a woman's breasts uncovered came to me in a flash of light in one of my early morning trips into the villages to the east with the bright morning sun in front. I stopped to let cross a troupe of Montagnard women walking from the village to town, most breasts still uncovered. And outlined in the early morning sun, a very pregnant woman was silhouetted in bright light. I was mesmerized. She moved as women do, proud and radiant. She smiled but did not look at me. I am sure she saw me glance at her. Her rounded pregnant-filled breasts seemed like such a natural part of life. In that moment, the typical male inquisitiveness about breasts vanished. Breasts became just another part of the female body whether any part is sexual is dependent on the context. I am ever grateful for that woman's presence, for her warm smile to help me out, for fear I would be gawking, distracted and disrespectful.

The next time I remember anything about breasts was almost two years later, when driving through a village, my eye caught a woman pounding rice. This, itself, was not unusual as pounding rice was woman's work. What caught my eye was the flash of the whiteness silhouetted against her otherwise naked deep brown body. She was wearing a bra. I felt concerned and saddened by what such a choice could mean for the future of these beautiful people, so much living with nature. All change requires deconstruction. Indeed, history is filled with the monuments of men and women who were creative destroyers of the "old way." And something new.

Even while helping the locals, the war was still on my mind. My journal on November 5, 1967, read: "—airlift—impending attack." On most nights, since my return to Kon Tum, my sleep had been disturbed by outbursts of mortar and machine gun fire from guard posts of military installations around Kon Tum. The sound from these outbursts came most loudly from the nearby airport garrisoned by South Vietnamese forces. Less loudly but quite distinctly, I could hear the popping sounds of outgoing mortar from MACV and Special Forces on the other side of town. It seemed the rapid fire of heavy machine guns and the occasional blast from heavy artillery came from everywhere. At night, all night, flares would shoot into the sky and slowly parachute to earth. Their reddish light against the black sky illuminated the movements of everything. As the flare slowly descended, its shadow cast on buildings and trees moved much more quickly than the sun's shadow, but still so slowly. In this eerie light, seeing slow-moving shadows and an overactive frightened imagination, I conjured menacing forms of death. I found these events unnerving, as did my housemate Joan. As by plan in case of attack, we would nervously and hastily leave our respective bedrooms, the top mattresses over our heads, as we moved quickly to the unfinished bathroom in the back of the house, away from the street. Sometimes we'd lay on the floor with mattresses on top of us and huddled, perhaps, somewhat physically closer than our relationship warranted. Watching and waiting in terror of death we never knew until the "firefight" had ended what the outcome would be.

I had been informed by Lieut. Tom D, a friend of Joan's, that these outbursts were based on army intelligence that indicated enemy forces would be "testing" the defense of the perimeters of Kon Tum. A real fight was coming. It was in the air. The fighters were still shadow boxing, getting ready for the real thing. I never knew whether these outbursts were triggered by an actual probe or whether tired and anxious guards sitting in high outposts in a state of war readiness were just oversensitive to any movement in the shadows of the dark perimeter. Shoot first and answer questions later as men on both sides of war were getting their "war nerves" for what was ahead.

The heightened state of war alerts was eroding my efforts to remain separate from the war. The very idea that I would not be on any side seemed illusory. The events of the next few weeks would fully explode this illusion.

On a night, the specific date I do not recall but sometime very soon after the security issue for civilians seem to be resolved, another "attack" made its noisy entrance into my sleep at my IVS house. Having gotten more used to the sounds of war, I was not quite so reactive; I remember quickly awaking only to be disturbed by a different sound. So much of war is sound. Listening to the sound can make the difference between survival and death. This different sound had a crunchy thud, followed almost instantly by a slight tremor of earth. Incoming and coming closer!

In war, the words "outgoing" and "incoming" have visceral meaning. While the sound of an outgoing ordinance can be disturbing to uninitiated nerves, there is reassurance to know that the hand of death is pointed away from you. Now, I was caught in the reality that the hand of death was pointed my way. My gut tightened, and the lump of lead in my stomach produced feelings of nausea. The bed began to shake. I jumped out of bed. I was shaken, and so was Joan as we huddled on the sofa, listening for the creeping effect that is the sound of an incoming landing nearer and nearer. This was before we put in place our better plan: at first signs of attack, we ran to the back of the house, each with mattresses over our heads to get away from the street.

What was even more alarming than these outbursts was the news that the Viet Cong were receiving rockets from the NVA supply line just to the west of Kon Tum. So, a lot of chatter about impending rocket attacks increased in strength.

This intelligence made Col. C nervous about our security. He was seriously considering pulling all civilians out of Kon Tum. At the very least, making us all sleep in the Kon Tum MACV compound. Apparently, he was dissuaded from pulling us all out by the bishop. But he was insisting civilians sleep in secured areas. By civilians, he was referring to Joan and myself, as well as the foreign staff of Minh Quy Hospital. All other civilian staff were in secured locations. When not at the hospital, the foreign staff resided at Patricia Smith's compound near my residence.

Dr. Patricia Smith was the guts of that mission hospital. She is a heroine whose story needs to be told. Pat felt in an awkward position because she relied on the good graces of the American presence for supplies; however, she was fiercely independent. Furthermore, she did not see the need to hide in MACV. I agreed with her logic, for when the attacks came, they were directed at the military compounds. Why sleep where the attacks would be directed? MACV commander Col. C was concerned about us being "outside the wire," in danger of capture or death. So, to keep in the good graces of the commander, we did sleep in MACV when he insisted (fearing an assault). And what Pat predicted came true. I can tell you, you ain't heard noise until you have a Viet Cong 122 mm rocket exploding in the bunk bed next door…he dies, you live. And it was only because the VC did not set all the rockets right to fire, for if all twenty had gone off, there would be not much left of the MACV. In the grand scheme of things, the attack on the MACV only caused slight damage. Lucky for us, this time. It is the terrifying noise of war embedded in my memory that can keep me awake at night, even now, fifty plus years on.

When not huddled together weathering these periodic attacks, I found myself looking forward to the evenings when Joan was not staying at Minh Quy. We talked and laughed. To my generally heavy intellectualized and rather plodding style, she was of good cheer, liked what she was doing, and danced with energy.

Through her, I became more involved with Minh Quy Hospital; first, by helping the gardener grow food for patients, and next, in bringing my considerable mechanical skills to bear on keeping the old, worn-out diesel generators running. Getting electricity to the hospital seemed a good thing. In fact, I began to wrestle with the idea of making the hospital more of my mission. IVS not too happy at first, having its two folks in Kon Tum focused on Minh Quy in what was essentially a Catholic Church-sponsored institution. On the other hand, Minh Quy was a hub to get services to beleaguered population. Sometimes love requires bending the rules to the greater good.

The hospital was financially dependent of the graces of Rome via the French Bishop in Kon Tum. I met with him several times. Always nice to stay in the good graces of the local bishop, and I made myself of use. I often acted on my trips between Kon Tum and Saigon, as courier for the Church. I carried everything from large amounts of money to precious medicines.

Regarding making Minh Quy more of my mission, Dr. Smith encouraged this; the need was there, and she was constantly shorthanded. The issue of state money going to support church activity was a subject of great discussion in IVS. All this resolved by the Tet Offensive of 1968, but that is for a later story.

The more involved I became with the hospital, the more Joan and I had to share. I quickly moved to a feeling about Joan that was beyond friendship. Perhaps because of the weird sense of time that was induced by culture shock in a war setting, November and December of 1967 seemed like a lengthy period of time. It was as if I had known Joan for a long time. Regardless, I do know that I felt drawn to her, and perhaps, I delude myself, but her to me as well. The reality was that she, like me, also felt more strongly connected to another. In her case, it was the man I replaced by coming to Kon Tum. This experience was confusing to me, feeling a deep connection to one woman while simultaneously feeling drawn to another. Life, as I had envisioned it, was not supposed to be this way. Back then in the fall of 1967, I began a journey that has led me to value the complexity and the wonder of love. At the time, it was only plain painful and confusing.

I may not recall the date of the attack, but I do recall the morning after another "test" of Kon Tum's defenses. Now, I was sleeping in my own place, and the nightly firefights were commonplace. I went up to the MAVC compound to get my mail per usual and maybe grab some breakfast. The red flag warning was up, and the mood was somber as I got my mail—they took several direct hits the night before. In my mind, this was further proof of why I did not want our team to sleep there. Vehicles were punctuated with shrapnel, tires flattened, and glass shattered. Some buildings damaged. I remember José, the civilian from Puerto Rico, bemoaning the damaged state of his brand-new International Scout. Transportation was hard to come by, and vehicle repair was slow as parts took forever and a day to arrive. I enjoyed José's sense of humor and good-naturedness; however, that morning he was glum. Apparently, he had been working hard on a project to restock fisheries. Kon Tum province was dotted with many fishponds; it seems each village had one, and José was about to embark on a project of seeding these ponds. Fish were a source of income and food. However, the attack had destroyed his transportation, but he had been told that it was too dangerous to drive the roads anyhow. So, he was in a quandary about how to proceed with this project. After exchanging some condolences about the fate of his life and project, he said he was going to take the day off. I knew he would be spending the better part of his day in his favorite brothel. If I wanted to find him, there he would be. I remember being surprised as business was always brisk.

The married men I talked to about their sex lives were not comfortable with what they did. They knew it was not right. Booze overcame their moral resistance. They were horny but mostly lonely for the comfort of a female body. The brothel was a place to relax. José, whatever his private thoughts about the morality of his acts may be, boasted of his feats. Every time he got a venereal disease, the penicillin injections were another "notch" on his belt. Literally. Showing his notched belt was his public boast, and he would show it laughing. He did not and could not understand my reticence to join him. Indeed, I was frequently the butt of much joking about my "Puritan" behavior. It was even implied that I might be queer. I did not really take offense, but I never liked that word either as it seemed to demean those who were queer.

To this day, I wonder how I might have been if I had a different kind of upbringing and values. All I know is that at the time, I saw their behavior as symbolic of how American policy made prostitutes of other cultures. Besides, I was so shy around women that I could never imagine myself relaxing enough to enjoy the experience. I still felt very Catholic in my moral objections to prostitution of any kind. Besides, I was poor. Even a couple of "cokes" in such a place would cost me a week's salary—cheap by American standards and expensive for my limited budget. There was no ATM, either.

Sometime during early November, I ran into Bill, a volunteer with Friends Services stationed at Đắk Tô 40 kilometers or so north on the major north–south axis in the Central Highlands, Vietnam. The other major north–south axis, a few clicks to the west, was the infamous Ho Chi Minh Trail named after the venerable and highly respected leader of North Vietnam. Bill had invited me up to see his site and the work he was doing. I mentioned this to my Vietnamese counterpart in the extension service. His boss, the Kon Tum agriculture chief, said my counterpart was to go with me to meet Bill.

So, one fine day in November, he and I headed north in my trusty and now well-running Scout. I remember him clearly. He was dressed in a light tan short-sleeved cotton shirt, Vietnamese-style loose trousers, sandals, and a pith hat. Our route was not paved—or, what was once pavement was pounded to dust by the American and South Vietnamese military convoys.

I had been used to seeing military convoys practicing for war. In my early years in Canada, during the time of the Korean War, the army would conduct convoys on our farm roads. I can remember trucks and tanks rumbling and mumbling up and down. When they stopped for a smoke, I was delighted if that occurred in front of our farm gate. I would walk among them. The men would be laughing, joking, and smoking with the kind of ease that comes from men being with men. But convoys in time of war…look out…

My first memory of an American convoy barreling through Kon Tum, heading north to engage the enemy, was a source of fright, anxiety, and exhilaration. I was standing about 200 feet from the main road on some errand to the American civilian compound just north of bridge. The ground shook under the weight of heavy tanks and fully loaded trucks with men and materials of war still many miles down the road. And the noise. Once across the river and past my view, tank drivers with heads appeared out of the driver's portal and atop each tank and vehicle, a fully loaded trigger finger was waiting for any reason to shoot. Each man was intensely watching for any sign of danger, engines screaming to the limit. The smell of dust and diesel and the sight of the omnipresent American flag. Some vehicles flew the Confederate flag. The convoy was always a roar and a rush barreling north to war.

One can only imagine the damage that such American convoys did to the roads in Vietnam. Deep potholes, huge ruts, some as deep as 2 feet, made driving a challenge. In wet season, it made such a mess. In the dry season, the potholes were so deep it made speed impossible. The impulse was to speed the myth to keep ahead of the blast. The road was periodically mined, and the Viet Cong were always about. Most of the road was nothing more than a strip of land cut primitively from the surrounding forest. At one point about halfway to Đăk Tô, I looked over at my passenger. He was sweating much more profusely than the heat of the day warranted. He was making the sign of the cross as we rounded each bend. I asked him if he was frightened. He looked nervously at me and said no, smiling. I did not believe him. I remained remarkably detached from the reality of the danger. I was in the middle of the battle for Đăk Tô, fall 1967, and I did not know it. But he did.

We arrived at Đăk Tô shortly after lunch. Bill had said that he would be easy to find as his house was on the main road to the left just inside the hamlet. And his vehicle, a brand-new British-built white Land Rover, out front for marker. Sure enough, the vehicle was there. We parked, got out, and walked to the vehicle where I could see it was severely damaged. Bill emerged from his small house, which was low down off the road embankment, looking tired and disheveled. Not like himself, always proper. During the previous night, the Viet Cong not only attacked the perimeter of the village but also came right through town down the main street. I can still see him pointing excitedly up and down the street, exclaiming that they were shooting into people's homes and lobbing a few hand grenades. Apparently, Bill's new Land Rover seemed an appropriate target, and so, someone lobbed a grenade into the front seat. I remember looking down at the driver's seat now in shreds, the windows shattered, the floor beneath the driver blown away, and the tires, at least the left front, was flat. To make a point of their displeasure at the sign of the foreigner, they shot into Bill's house. On hearing the noise, Bill had rolled under his bed. I could see where bullets slammed through wall just above where he lay under his bed.

Remarkably, Bill seems pretty nonplussed and still wanted very much to show us his work in the fields around Đăk Tô. I can still feel the afternoon sun warm on my face walking through fields, kicking the soil, and seeing the dust in the wind. I felt at peace with my new life—at least, in those couple of hours wandering around this beautiful country. The fact that war was everywhere seemed odd and incongruous.

As we departed Đắk Tô, so was an American convoy traveling south to Pleiku through Kon Tum. It made no sense to ride ahead of them or be last, so I pushed my way into the convoy, not moving too fast. Nearer the middle was the safest bet, I thought. This would be my first experience of many traveling inside a large convoy. We were always encouraged to do this as a way of avoiding mines and capture. Needless to say, my ambivalence about doing this was great as it seemed like the ultimate compromise to my mission. However, on this day, ambivalence be dammed. The safest way south before dark (even I did not risk the roads at night except within city limits) was to make our way south in this convoy. Perhaps because we were heading south and away from the fighting up north of Đắk Tô, or perhaps because it was just too large to move too fast, the pace south was more relaxed than a northbound convoy. I relaxed and began to enjoy, even laughed to myself about the craziness of it all.

Suddenly, we stopped. The sounds of war were upon us. Men started jumping out of vehicles, throwing on flak jackets and helmets, clutching furiously at their M-16s. "Get out, get in the ditch" the lieutenant in the vehicle behind me barked in my ear upon seeing me sitting momentarily stunned. I remember jumping and crouching in the shallow ditch filled with other men. As my ear pressed on the ground, I could both feel and hear the sounds of war exploding into my consciousness.

Time was frozen in eternity to hear nothing except the screaming from the hell of war. I was imprisoned in the terror of noise. Yet, I could still see the world around me. Men next to me, trained though they were, seemed just as terrified as me. The smell of fear. The ground shook as heavy ordinance slammed into the earth itself nearby. In that moment, it occurred to me Mother Earth is not just a stage for war but feels the hot blasts of fire on her skin.

As I took the chance to look up, as others were, I could see a small battle going on about 500 meters to my left about 11 o'clock at the base of a large hill—one of many battles in the mountainous regions of the Vietnamese Highlands. I could see and hear American Air Force planes strafing the upper part of the hill as the upper part of the hill rained death down on us. I could see puffs of smoke on the hillside as men of both sides engaged each other.

I had come to appreciate the beauty of this part of Vietnam. Perhaps, my mind remembers falsely, but I do recall many beautiful greens on slopes and the country hillside filled with small rivers and streams. It seemed like there was month after month of beautiful days. In dry season, the days were hot and clear with reasonably cool nights, even 50°F. How cold that felt. Then came the rainy humid season, and while it rained a lot and was humid, it was never as tropical as Saigon. It was a beautiful part of the world.

But not that day. Lying in a ditch, I was initiated into another phase of what turned out to be another on-the-job basic warfare training; I was getting my "war nerves." Maybe an hour or so, perhaps a break in the fighting…and then all clear. I don't remember much of the rest of that afternoon. Later, much later, near dusk, crawling into Kon Tum, I remember feeling grateful to be alive. I noticed blood dried on the left side of my face…the world has looked different to me since that long afternoon. Surely, humans can do better than war? Why not justice as the Holy Books command? Seemed worth a shot.

My diaries reflect that I was focused on many inner struggles not so cerebral. I was feeling confronted by the horrifying picture of war that was emerging and the experience of being pulled by the attraction, the invitation, and the beauty of two women. The pull to Luisa was strong and would always be the center of my heart. However, I could feel myself splitting as I wrestled with the age-old problems of triangular relationships. It is a problem that only gets resolved in the paradox of the triune forces of love that bring us into existence.

The buzz of all this inner and outer activity was broken up by Christmas. From communications with IVS-Saigon, I learned that I was to make my way to Buôn Mê Thuột for an all Vietnam team meeting. IVS was congregating in the hope that a Christmas truce would hold. It was like a vacation, but it had a purpose: morale building, sharing ideas and supporting each other in our efforts. The truce held. Other than a few nervous fingers the first night…the sounds of war were silent. What a blessing. And what a blessing when war is done forever.

The first night of our team meeting, we slept under large tents. I have the memory of being so cold, sleeping on army cots with only one blanket in temperatures far below what my tropically-conditioned body could tolerate. I spent the night shivering—not wanting to disturb anybody but desperately wanting heat—imagining someone's body heat would have been nice, but I was too afraid to ask.

In those days, I discovered IVS was populated with a host of characters, all engaging, witty, friendly, and knowledgeable. Steve (My CIA finger at Harper's Ferry) is not among my memories of that experience. He was already disaffected with IVS as he communicated to me in a visit to Kon Tum in early December...he was looking for something else to do. I am still haunted by images of him, of how he changed. I remember meeting him at Kon Tum airport, the pacifist now gun carrying, fearful, and not at all his extroverted, left-leaning, outspoken self. I wondered what happened, and then I remembered I too carried guns in certain situations. I was trained to use them as a matter of requirement if I wanted to hitch a ride in convoys...war does that to you.

A memory: on one of my trips back from Saigon to Kon Tum, I got stuck in the middle of the jungle. I have no memory of what happened to the "chopper" I was on that put me in this situation. I can still see myself standing on the side of road, which was very muddy. It was a wet and dreary early morning. I was carrying money for the bishop, and I had time sensitive medicines I had to get to Minh Quy by noon. I remember walking up to the passenger-side door of a large semi...the engine at idle, a convoy getting ready to roll north. I banged on the door and heard a grunt. I opened it. I looked up into cab and saw the passenger seat was open. I asked for a ride north to Kon Tum. The driver eyed me suspiciously and pointed to an M-16 beside my intended seat. In a slow drawl and point of finger, he asked, "do you know how to use that?" I choked a little. I am sure he saw it. I nodded yes, he nodded back, and in I climbed, and off we went...M-16 pointed out the window.

My shock at Steve's changes were really just an image of myself in the mirror that I could only see dimly.

My strongest memory of that Christmas truce was the good time I had with N, Joan's significant other. I felt conjoined with him in making the pit-roasted pig, which was the highlight of our time at the team gathering. He was Hawaiian and was in charge, a natural leader. The digging of the pit, the gathering of rocks and firewood, cooking the pig, the group ritual. A Hawaiian lu'au was the central focus of the partying and dancing until almost dawn.

That night, after the partying was done, there was quietness. No ordinance was fired. The guns were silent. I had not realized, as I stared into the starry night, just how quietness can be so wonderful. How much there that is positive, pure, and holy when you listen to silence. And, how terrifying that silence can be when you feel unsafe and threatened. My overindulgence was a little too much alcohol. I remember awaking the second morning with my head on a log next to slumbering fire pit shared by N and others. It wasn't cold that night. The heat from the rocks felt wonderful as did the heat of the morning sun.

A Siesta Visitor, November 1967

In what I remember as early mid-November, a Vietnamese boy of about twelve knocked on my door at the end of siesta. Siesta, what a wonderful idea: a real break in the middle of the heat of day.

The boy talked in broken English and pointed to a young woman standing on the roadside. She was his sister. He was asking me to their parent's house, where I was to meet them and be introduced to her. I understood that proper protocol required me to not acknowledge her until I had been formally introduced.

Her parent's motives for wanting me to teach their daughter English remains unclear to me unto this day. I understood from cultural training classes that Vietnamese women, particularly young and unmarried, who interacted with the enemy were viewed as consorting with something unclean and sullied by association within their own culture. The willingness of Vietnamese women to associate with Americans, whatever the intent and motivation may be, was a cultural surprise to me. Since that time, reflecting upon the nature of humankind, I now wonder if these women were not doing their part to make peace with the foreigner...a kind of deeper reproductive code surfacing in human behavior. And perhaps it was also within the American's deeper, unconscious instinctual needs as well. The children born from these unions is, as I understand it, to this day a problem in Vietnamese society.

I observed that foreign men in substantial numbers entered various kinds of relationships with Vietnamese women—consented and willingly, married or not, whatever their conscious intention and motivation. In truth though, a high percentage of the sexual contacts would be of a forced nature, even onto rape. If the Japanese apologized for their use of "comfort women" during war, shouldn't Americans do the same?

In truth, it was the exceptional American male who did not have some sexual contact with a Vietnamese woman at some point. Where there were Americans, "steam baths" and "bars" were there in large numbers. For the Vietnamese, the provisioning of these services was a way to make money and gather intelligence. These sexual services, tacitly supported by official American authority to satisfy the sexual appetites of men, were shut down when high-ranking authorities came to inspect the forces. From my observations, loneliness and boredom were the prime factors in motivating patronage. Some of these "bars" did indeed create a sense of safety and home, however false. I believe the superior intelligence gathered in these settings, and the accurate handling and processing of this information, was a major factor in the Communist's success. I constantly remembered the first thing a Vietnamese man said to me upon entering Vietnam, "Remember, a nation at war with itself is a nation of spies." He was from the north. To this day, I wonder if he was one of those spies, so many of which I would later encounter. It was spies on both sides who I came to rely upon in order to stay alive; although, I did not think about such things at the time. I did what I needed to do to stay alive. It was more instinctual. There were times when I made pacts with the devil...it seemed so even at that time. I ask forgiveness. War is evil, the devil personified. I know his sound.

Was I about to make myself part of some scheme that could bring harm to this woman? Was I a pawn in a larger struggle? This was my state of mind as I followed her as she rode gracefully poised on the back of her brother's motorcycle. Her long black hair and *ao dai*[7] was streaming in the wind. From the cut of her hair and clothing, I knew her family was from the north and probably Catholic. Surviving is about intelligence. I wondered if they knew I was Roman Catholic. A nation in civil war is a nation of spies, I remembered.

---

[7] Vietnamese style of dress worn mostly by women.

I forgot for a moment about traditional customs, and I asked through her brother for her to ride with me in my pale yellow old American army jeep. And felt stupid for asking—how quickly I became unconscious and reverted to improper American behavior. But at least I remembered not to look directly at or speak to her. I felt both excited and a little scared knowing that I had been observed as a "safe man;" I was on the verge of accomplishing one of my first goals in Vietnam—entry into Vietnamese society. Whatever my concerns and fears, I was moving forward.

The parents wanted me to teach their daughter English. In exchange, I could practice my Vietnamese, in their beautiful and very upscale French stone villa. I formally met my student, Miss Q, after being sized-up by her parents. Over tea, I agreed to meet with their daughter twice weekly for an hour. Tuesdays and Thursdays, after siesta. I could practice my Vietnamese with her, but the focus was on her learning to speak English.

In our meetings, we conversed about everyday things: my family, her family, the weather, but never war. Her brother always present. And then, the Tet Offensive of 1968 came in full fury and ended that.

I went back to their home after Tet. Their beautiful home was a victim of war and the family was nowhere to be seen. I have often wondered where the story of me and Miss Q might have gone if that relationship continued. I have imagined engaging a writer, perhaps Vietnamese, to project herself into that time to tell their story, an imagination based on this introduction in real time. And so, the story of Miss Q and JanStephen will perhaps one day emerge[8].

---

[8] I thank my niece Kari for the fun of starting to tell their story.

Purple Heart Incident, Late Fall 1967

March 29, 2020: In the process of writing about my time in Vietnam, I recovered memories as I peeled back the time. In reading those journals now, I noticed how I made little mention of what was really going on...on the ground.

All these years later, there is still a telltale, barely visible, vertical scar in the middle of my left eyebrow. In the morning mirror as I shave, I see the scar fading, after all these years. Immediately, I am taken back, sometime in late fall 1967...

I was at the civilian American compound, a few hundred feet on northeast side of the river, near the bridge over Đắk Bla River. The bridge was heavily guarded with outposts clearly in view from where I stood. It was midafternoon on a cloudy day. I must have heard a convoy coming...and what became an almost daily mad rush of men and machines off to war headed north...heard long before seen.

And ever a sight to see as I was standing outside at the corner of the compound building. I had every intent to watch, but I also had a sense of needing cover. So, I carefully peeked around the corner of the building. I remember a terrifying rush of sound, of heavy machine gun fire so close by. The shock waves of the sound hit me. In terror, I flattened myself against the corner of the building, hurdling myself into the hard corner of wood. I can still feel it. With such force, it gave me a gash above my left eyebrow. I was stunned, but all right.

Later that afternoon, I remember sitting in the officer mess hall at MACV for drinks and dinner. Col. C, upon seeing my wounded eye and blood still on my shirt, said "You should get a Purple Heart." I was somewhat flabbergasted...to be so identified, it was a bit of a shock. I smiled an awkward *thank you* and said no.

Reflecting on that time, I wish I had said yes. For sure, I would have been denied, but at least, there would have been a paper trail. The only physical proof I have now of my time in that war is a barely visible vertical scar in the middle of my left eyebrow, now fading away.

Preview Tet, January 1968

A month before "it" broke, Jhar, my main contact with the Bahnar people, gave me his guns for safe keeping. He said, "I do not want them in my house when they come."

I learned upon my return to Kon Tum during Tet '68 that they came and killed him.

I do not know how to describe the horror of going into a smoldering Montagnard village the morning after a VC attack. In my mind's eye, I can still see whole families burned to death, their blackened skeletons and fleshless skulls with mouths open in screams of pain, frozen in time. Families huddled together in terror under their stilted homes, frying to death. If they ran away, the enemy killed them. War is hell. Why some survive and others do not…these too are the mysteries of war.

The Americans were no better with their free-fire zones and their "tiger prison[9]." I was even present once as VC soldiers were thrown out of helicopter to prompt the others. I can still see the terror in their eyes as they were tossed from the side of the Huey, the look of horror on those who remained. Who would be next? Sometimes I feared in the frenzy of killing that I would be next. As a civilian traveling with officer status, I was often considered to be only a step away from being the enemy.

Civil war is a particularly dirty kind of war. What brother will do to brother!

---

[9] A prison on Côn Sơn island where some prisoners were kept in tiger cages.

January 3, 1968, Kon Tum

From my diary notes on this day, I wrote *security issues on the perimeter of Kon Tum. Pender and L dead. K's village overrun* projects *are ruined.*

This was the situation that greeted my return to Kon Tum from our IVS Christmas break. The truce held, but the next day, the killing began again in earnest. Pender, an American soldier, and L, his Montagnard interpreter, were on their way out to a village that I had visited many times. They hit a landmine. Although, I did not know this man personally, I felt like I did. The sense was that it could have been me. I dealt with his death by some combination of denial, rationalization, and plain stupidity. I kept driving to villages.

American activity tended to be very predictable. So perhaps, the VC knew that Pender and L were going out there that day and decided this was the day to make a statement. My own activities were unpredictable; plus, I assumed the VC knew who I was and that I was neutral in my intent. This is quite an assumption. The only indicator that this might have been true was the signals I used to get from Jhar that certain villages were off-limits on certain days. He knew what was going on and was using his knowledge to keep me safe. In addition, I rationalized, I traveled backroads rarely used by Vietnamese or American government or military personnel. These "roads" were more like wide paths of sand through the bush. Besides, if you drove over 35 miles per hour, the mine went off behind you. Or at least, that was the rumor. I never found anyone who could personally verify this, but I took some comfort in this and drove as fast as I could over very rough terrain.

1/10/1968

In the months since my August arrival in Kon Tum, day by day, a peculiar tension mounted. And by night, I could feel a quickened pulse of war. My housemate and I would still grab our top mattress and run to the back of the house, mattress over heads. I can still see her coming out of her room, the white flashes of explosions silhouetting her body and the mattress over her head. We were scurrying to the cement enclosed "bunker" at the back of the house, which was in an unfinished shower area. As far from the street as possible. I counted the seconds between light and sound; the timing of blasts indicated incoming ordnance within one thousand yards and closing. The incoming was like lightning: the closer the time between light and sound, the closer to death.

For much of the fall, this was almost a twice-a-week ritual. Most times, we would sit side by side, backs to the inner walls, knees under chins, and mattresses upright as a cover, like a triangular tent. Most nights, we could hear a few shells of incoming rockets and a barrage of outgoing fire, as well as all kinds of sounds from guns. And always, the sound of Huey choppers, their unique sound of rotor blades slapping and snapping the air, racing off into the night.

Most nights, we were back in bed in an hour or two. However, January 10, 1968, was different.

Through most of that night, Joan and I lay under the mattresses piled on top of each other, burying ourselves into the hard floor to be as flat as possible, wanting to sink into the tile. We lay in terror as the noise and utter chaos of war roiled about us. Our arms around one another, she spoke to me in those moments of terrifying silence (the terror of silence in war is worse than the noise) of what she wanted me to know if I should survive and not her. She made me promise to tell her family and lover her dying words. Before the night was out, I had done the same.

At dawn, we stood arm and arm on the porch, watching women and men balance their loads of chattel on long poles over their shoulder, bouncing along in the great silence that follows the raging of war.

I can still see and feel the peace I felt that next morning just for being alive.

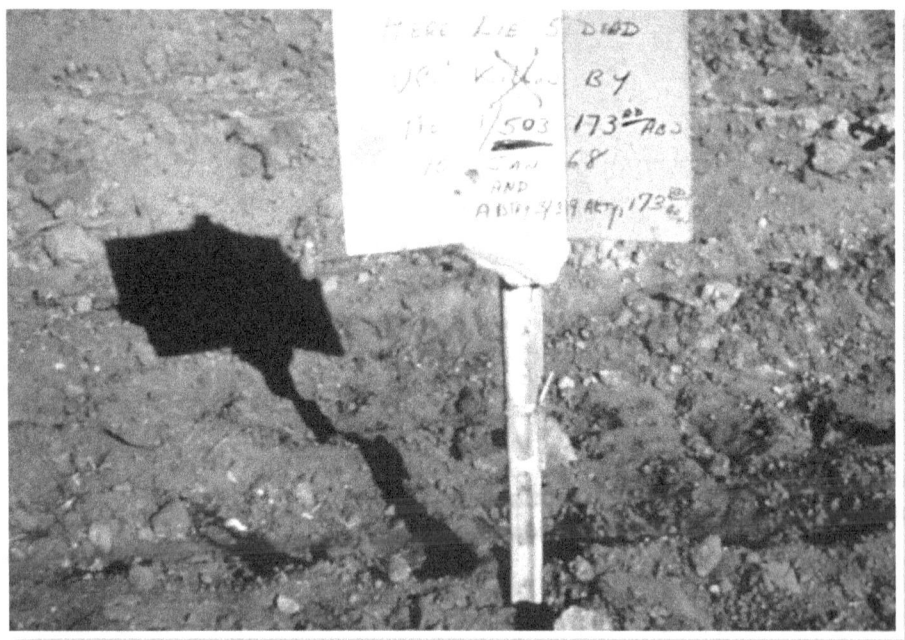

And now, as I remember that feeling to put words to my thinking, "War is barbarism."

Commentary on Journal Entry, January 14, 1968

What strikes me as so odd about this journal entry, as I look back, is that there is no mention of January 10, a night of terror that only one other knows. Joan.

Instead, in my journals I write about my "crisis" of mission without much acknowledgment of what happened only four days earlier. Not so odd, I guess, as denial is among the one of the most prime defense mechanisms. You either live or die. I was detached from the brutality of my reality.

My notes indicate reflections on my dependence on contact with Vietnamese and work within the culture. I noted that my effort to teach English to Miss Q was sporadic. The reasons were partly due to my schedule. It was rice planting season, and part of my mission was to demonstrate the new mechanical wet rice tillers—Japanese made diesel engines. They were designed to replace the water buffalo. I also, as farm boy, went through the transition from animal to tractor, so I understood the meaning of this change; now, I was doing it on the other side of the world.

The war decided things for me. The plight of the Montagnard became my top focus. The alleviation of their suffering from war was begetting a great need.

I have some particularly horrifying memories of Montagnard coming onto hospital grounds severely wounded by unexploded ordinances. I remember one particularly gruesome incident of a boy of about ten, walking into the hospital yard, showing me his hands and arms and seeing his fingers…just all bone. Flesh completely blown off his arms, and off to the American hospital army tent across the bridge we went. Not a tear or a whimper out of him—in shock, I guess.

And for sure, my sense of mission was also complicated by issues of safety. In Kon Tum province, all of the roads were mined periodically by the Viet Cong, so each trip over any road was like playing Russian roulette. I was always afraid on the roads, but this did not stop me from driving on them. The Americans thought I was crazy. Going to the helipad to get comrades and friends wounded or killed by road mines was a common experience. I lived in a bubble, or so it seemed. But, I made it known to the locals that I was Canadian and not in favor of the American War. I was here to help. It is only through luck or some greater design that I am still here.

Letters to Luisa, Tet '68

January 18, 1968, 10 a.m.

My Dearest Louisa,

I am in Nha Trang with my team. The VC has been giving all of us in Kon Tum a rough time. I decided to bring them here for safety...authorities are not happy with my decision as it makes them look bad. It does; our leaders are in denial. I shall not go into all the gory details. But because of the security situation, most of the villages I have worked in have been hit hard. Also, the training center was destroyed, and the road to it is quite insecure. The end of the training center as part of my mission. The enemy is closing in.

    I have desired a change of job emphasis. I will speak to the team and regional leaders about that.

* * *

January 31, 1968, 1:30 p.m.

My Darling Louisa,

I am in Saigon in a hospital, and there is a bloody war going on right up the street. Now to begin at the beginning—if I am intelligible.

I was ordered back to Saigon because word got out that yours truly was taking horrible risks, and there were concerns that Kon Tum was about to be overrun. Overall, our security was in question when one of our IVS team was shot and killed by the Viet Cong—or ARVN?[10] Our efforts to be neutral as a team can make us unpopular with everyone.

So, about a week ago, I drove my trusty Scout onto the back of army transport plane (a Caribou flown by Australians fearlessly crazy) from Kon Tum and flew with it to Tan Son Nhut in Saigon. And then I drove the Scout to IVS headquarters. Fastest time ever between those two destinations! Sometime in the next couple of days…I remember feeling quite unwell. I remember looking down as I urinated, noticing the pain and being quite concerned when my urine was iridescent green. *Not good.*

I remember being taken to a French hospital accompanied by IVS friends and staff to be admitted. I remember feeling very, very unwell. I lost track of time. I remember standing naked in a toilet closet off main hall…no door…fluids coming out of all orifices at once…including eyes and ears. I cannot remember the misery I felt. I was in isolation. Probable diagnosis: typhoid fever. Turns out that wise old French doctor, having seen it a lot, got it right enough and saved my life. But it was late to treat, so the disease advanced…to suffer.

I remember being told that evening, on what turned out to be the eve of Tet '68, that I might not make it to morning and to say my prayers. No priest. Sometime in the night, I remember a loud and sustained popping noise in background…I did not understand what was happening (Tet is celebrated with millions of

---

[10] South Vietnamese Army

firecrackers). Whether fever, dream, or reality, I do not know…in the middle of the night, I saw a soldier with a gun in darkened doorway, pointing it at me. I could see his toothy mouth in the dim light as he turned away. Perhaps seeing my skeleton so near to death, he decided not to waste a bullet on me. God's mercy!

I was awakened at dawn by those all too familiar sounds of war: mortar and machine gun not far away. A lot. Seemed both friendly and hostile. I was aware immediately that I was going to live…my fever broke. I turned a corner in the night. Those of us deeply sick know that feeling of a corner turned. Still half-asleep, half-drugged, and believing I was in Kon Tum, I look out my window. In the empty street below, a single NVA soldier was walking down the street. I thought that odd. I can still see the helmet, tan shorts, and tall boots and gun. I startled awake to run and awoke Joan. I ran into the edge of half-opened door and got some sense.

I have heard a lot of rumors about what's going on, but I know no reliable source here—you may know more than me.

I am in bad shape.

Naturally, I haven't gotten mail from you in ages, so I hope you are well. I do recall in one card, something about a card "to immortalize me." Time to rest again.

* * *

Same letter, February 2, at a hotel in downtown Saigon:

> Hi again, by now you well know the seriousness of the situation here. I am in the middle of it all.
>
> On the morning of the first, I was discharged from the French hospital. The place was full of people seriously injured by the war. I grabbed a three-wheel taxi to the IVS house only to find it abandoned and with unmistakable evidence of battle zone damage. So, my driver, dodging roadblocks, snipers, and battle zones, brought me to the temporary IVS headquarters, a large hotel downtown.

As I begin to feel better, I become more conscious of what's going on. Kon Tum has been overrun, which comes as little surprise, except that I now wish I knew who is dead and alive.

No mail is going out these days, so you probably figured out that I have been in Kon Tum and know it was overrun and wondering my fate. I don't know how many days I will be here. It's amazing to see the streets of Saigon vacant during the day. There still is a lot of bombing, and Radio America tells we are winning the war. That's good, but we are still locked up in this bloody hotel and we are running out of food.

God, I would be glad to hear from you.

I love you,
Jan

* * *

After being discharged from the local hospital, I was given strenuous warnings to take it easy or trigger relapse. I did not take it easy and can still remember the director screaming at me for being so active. And sure enough, I relapsed.

This time, I was admitted to American Military Field Hospital in Saigon. They all were puzzled as to my symptoms, and so I was sent off to isolation and many, many tests to confirm the French doctor's diagnosis to discover it was murine typhus that brought me so low. And lucky they caught it when they did they said, or it would be unlikely I survived. And for sure, that disease damn near killed me, as dead in this war as with a bullet. How did this dreaded disease come upon me?

My best guess: In one of my trips between Kon Tum and Saigon, only not by Air America, but US military flights through Cam Ranh Bay, and often the last stretch into Kon Tum by helicopter. One night, we got stuck on a hilltop outpost at an old French fort for the night. The helicopter ran into some bullets and needed to land quickly. Now, that was a trip down fast as I perched in the turret with the gunner. They expected to patch it up and be off to Kon Tum come morning. I remember sleeping on the sand in that old French fort, my back curled against a cement wall in a corner of the turret. This illness is born by the fleas of rats, and I remember black rats crawling on me that night.

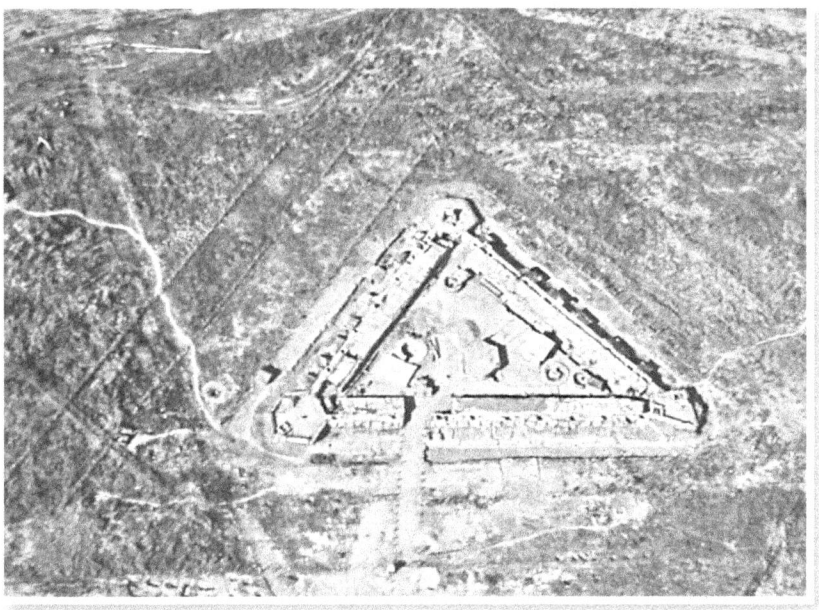

Note: There was even a letter sent from State Department to let my parents know that I was missing in action during Tet '68, a subject that my mother and I had difficulty acknowledging even into her dying days. The letter was so painful that she tore it up.

Post Tet 1968, Transition from International Voluntary Services to Catholic Relief Services

The story of transitioning my services from IVS centers around the outcome of the Tet Offensive and the countrywide insecurity. Upon post-Tet evaluation of countrywide security, IVS decided to downsize, and Kon Tum was on the chopping block. What would be my outcome?

Many volunteers were sent home. IVS wanted me to stay and offered me a more secure station at Buôn Ma Thuột. I checked it out...it seemed quiet, but in truth, I felt tired and did not know if I had the energy to start over in an unknown place. In the meantime, as I was in Saigon, I met Steve over dinner, and he mentioned he planned to leave IVS. He noted that Catholic Relief Services (CRS) was looking to hire team leaders. Through a government contract, CRS had been able to provide teams of nurses and community development folks at ten sites in Vietnam. He thought I was a suitable candidate. In his mind, IVS's philosophy was useless in a country at war...so pick a side and make some money. War had really made Steve a cynic. I remembered our conversations on nonviolence and pacifism at Harper's Ferry...and how far barely six months of war had turned our heads around.

Looking for something different, I met with CRS to check out the details, and sure enough, Kon Tum was on their list for a team leader. It took much back and forth on the part of all parties for reasons of little importance, just bureaucracy being bureaucracy. In the end, I was offered a team leader position with CRS for the Kon Tum situation. I was drawn by my background and fate back into the lion's den.

Sometime in late spring 1968, I left Saigon with my team of four women. We traveled Air America, the usual route. Three of them were nuns, two nurses, and one technician—later to be called Sister Shit (looking at feces under telescope was pretty much her job description). The fourth was a civilian trained in nutrition. The first problem I faced was finding a suitable team residence as we were under the gun to get on the ground and get running. The team's permanent residence, a large three-story structure, very bright pink in the center of town, was not yet ready. I was told that at one time, it was the CIA headquarters. Whether that was true or not, I hoped that the enemy had updated intelligence... women, nuns no less, were now in residence. I took some hope that nuns would keep us safer.

Until that residency opened downtown, we found residence in a large home on the outskirts of Kon Tum. The top of the underground bunker became my bed. Though we were feeling rather exposed on the edge of the woods, we were glad to get closer to center of town and greater security.

I Destroyed It to Save It

A memory: I am standing beside Captain J. We each have tears in our eyes as we survey a Vietnamese village he had been ordered to destroy during the night. In our eyes, we gather in the horror of the aftermath that his command had wrought. Animals slaughtered, huts burned to the ground, and women, children, and old men in bits and parts, everywhere. The smell of war and death are the stillness after the war, the earth red with the bright rising sun. Standing in the cool morning sun, I can see steam rising from decaying bodies. Captain J said that he was ordered to destroy it to save it.

There I stood with my friend and drinking buddy, the person who many times debated the question: Was this war an example of "just war" theory in practice? As now, we stood locked in a time and place where the theory of war and practice of peace met the reality of war. We walked sadly away. As usual, war won.

There are those who believe it is right to destroy to save, and there are those who will carry out orders to enact that belief. The village that my friend was ordered to destroy as a man of war was the village that I had come to as a man of peace to assist with quality of living. I had had some success in this village. The water quality improved; rice production went up; and mechanization was introduced. I knew everyone. Now, all gone in the name of war. Just two weeks before, I had witnessed the aftermath of NVA-burned Montagnard village. Images of screaming bodies trapped under their homes burning to death haunts me to this day. Each side's heroes were doing the dirty work as such is the nature of guerrilla warfare. Whether it be Vietnam 1968 or now, nothing has changed except the scale of the catastrophe ahead.

And as I read these words now as I write…I think them truer.

Man makes stupid plans, and God laughs.

Renata Captured

March 8, 1968

My Dearest Louisa,

God, what a rough week, with all the packing to end IVS Kon Tum. And then the VC capture of one of the nurses from Minh Quy Hospital. We had to move the hospital closer to town to make it safer…the enemy is not far away.

Back on that night with Joan and I hiding under mattresses in the IVS house, once again in the hopes that the shockwaves nearby of rockets wouldn't kill us, there was another drama going on about a kilometer away at Minh Quy. Renata K, a German volunteer nurse, was captured in the night by the VC. We assumed they came looking for Pat Smith and by mistaken identity took Renata. Bad intelligence. Whatever, Minh Quy was now too insecure, so the following days were spent helping Pat move the hospital to a new location closer to town. Pat suffered the loss not only of Renata, but also shortly after, the two other Danish nurses' contracts naturally expired. They were eager to get out of town. To fill the vacuum, CRS was in the process of putting contract nurses into Minh Quy.

It became clear to me that Kon Tum was really going to be a mess unless someone took personal interest in it. I made the decision to leave IVS and I was offered Kon Tum team leader position by CRS, and I accepted. This action pleased the director, for now he could please the bishop, but it displeased the program coordinator, who thought Kon Tum was a bad idea. His opinion is not without merit! Although, the program coordinator knew that he would be overruled by the director on orders from the bishop. Hell be damned, there would be a Kon Tum CRS team.

I braced to do the best we could. The exact complexities and overall situation I will deal with another time. The bottom line: A letter of understanding has been worked out between me and the director. Pat Smith has a statement that the team leader assigned to Kon Tum "has complete jurisdiction over the CRS team."

I am now living in my new Saigon villa apartment when I'm not in Kon Tum.

I love you, Louisa.
Jan

May 15, 1968, North of Kon Tum

My Dearest Love,

It is about noon, and I am sitting on the hood of a jeep on the side of a hill, overlooking a beautiful valley about ten klicks north of Kon Tum. The temp is about 94 degrees. The sun is hot and the air is very heavy with water. The Vietnamese soldier standing beside the vehicle is sweating profusely, wondering, I presume, if some rain will come tonight to break the heat.

I'm up here in the Highlands laying groundwork for the CRS team, and because I was visiting the American adviser in the area, I was invited along with him to attend the opening ceremonies of a bridge and spillway project completed. I sit overlooking the beautiful valley with the bright blue sky and fluffy clouds. I hear in the distance the thumping of guns, the roar of tanks, and a few minutes ago, someone opened up a 50-caliber machine gun so close, the reverberations shake the ground.

But all is well as I sit here. Across the small river below me and to my right, about thirty functionaries for the South Vietnam government sit under a blue parachute that they are using for shade. They are perfect targets, but everyone eats. The children sing government songs. The women gather about and watch. The wind rustles the tall grass—I think it is going to rain.

I love you so very much.
Jan

Deep Agent, Fred

In a letter to a dear friend in Canada, I told the story of Fred B:

First, some context. My organization was called International Voluntary Services (IVS), the forerunner of the Peace Corp. Whereas the Peace Corp would not accept "third country nations," IVS would take me (a Canadian). It required college educated people. IVS was "people development focused." The idea was to go to underdevelopment nations and to offer help *within* the context of the culture in which we worked. The idea was not to export Western ideas "wholesale" but take what was best and make them work within the context of the culture. Digging a well, using fertilizers, pest control, general farming technology to improve food production, or teaching how to repair an engine...all of this done carefully to respect the integrity of the people.

My job was to bring that kind of knowledge to Kon Tum and the surrounding area through the Agricultural Extension Program, which was part of the South Vietnamese government outpost in Kon Tum. The American Army had its own "hearts and minds program" in winning the guerrilla war with their own agricultural/development teams. I very much did my own program according to the principles I had been taught...it was also political to meet and be in touch with the Americans who worked for USAID.

It was in the context of helping an agent from that program that I got to "command" a Huey helicopter. That was a wild experience. My USAID counterpart in agriculture had to leave town and needed someone to complete the seeding of the province-wide fishpond seeding project. Roads were insecure, so the task was to be done by helicopter. I agreed to do it. The pilots, fresh from battle near Đắk Tô, were under orders to assist in the fish-seeding pond mission. I often wondered what the pilots thought, to go in one hour from killing the motherfuckers and the next to feeding the motherfuckers! They were to descend and hover over village ponds as I told them where to drop the seed fish as I hung over the side of helicopter. They thought I was nuts, and they were surely glad to see the last of me.

A major theme and tension for me in Vietnam was how to maintain a cooperative affiliation with the Americans and yet not compromise myself in the eye of the Vietnamese, many of whom were highly sympathetic to the Viet Cong. To me, they were not the enemy…they were just people fighting a war they believed in, and I did not hide the fact that I was sympathetic to their cause. Who wants invaders? I did not hide my sentiments about the illegality of the war from my American friends when such debate felt safe to have. I lied to no one. I was trustable. I was one of the people who met the Viet Cong when they handed over the German nurse captured by the Viet Cong one year after her capture.

My, what a story she had to tell. Imagine you are a nurse on night duty in a war that is noisy every night, nerves on edge. Then, the enemy comes storming in, and, fearing for your life, you're not killed but captured. She experienced the hellish terror of war firsthand and then survived a year in the jungle living with them. She told us she was treated with respect. She said the hardest thing was not having female hygiene products. The most fearful thing was the B-52 bombings in the middle of the night.

Treated with respect. I remember her telling me this and then remembered the American propaganda effort to get her back…dropping leaflets from the sky, promising reward for her release, intelligence officials speculating she was being used as a VC whore. Projection, I thought.

Many in the CIA became good friends of mine. They wondered how I could move about so freely and come back alive. Wondered if I knew more of what was going on than I was saying. And would feed them intelligence to keep in their good graces. Like the time a formation of NVA passed in front of me on a road east of Kon Tum. By the time I told them, the formation of NVA has passed on, but I was still giving my CIA colleagues intelligence on enemy presence and number. A win-win in my morality.

It was in this context that I met Fred B, near the end of my tour in the early spring of 1969. Every now and again, I would attend one of the American's Saturday nights get togethers for the civilian types at MACV. Lots to drink, plenty of American food, and later, a strip show. At that get-together, Fred approached me...I remember his lanky all-American good looks and easy charm. I liked him immediately. It was one of those moments when you meet someone and take an instant liking to them even before much is said. We became buddies. I liked his intelligence, good humor, and his clear understanding of the issues we were facing. We talked of work projects and agreed to get together and share ideas. We did some collaboration.

What was most unusual about Fred was we could talk politics and philosophy, indicating his elevated level of education. What was more unusual was that he spoke fluent Vietnamese. It flowed off his tongue like music. He was not your typical USAID consultant. Competent, but narrowly schooled. I wonder now if he was a deep agent, blending in to check me out...and I guess gained his trust.

Later, after I returned to the US, now married, I received an "urgent" call in the middle of the night in 1971 from Hawaii. On the phone: It was him. How would he even have my number? He was on his way back to Vietnam as the war was winding down, he said. He asked me...a high-valued asset was to be pick up at the airport in Boston, a Vietnamese woman...and to be delivered to an address in Connecticut. Would I do it?

I agreed. Luisa and I together shepherded her to that location.

I remember getting off the phone call and wondering if this was Fred finally revealing himself as the deep agent.

Recollections: Minh Quy Hospital and Jeff

Minh Quy Hospital was under the charge of Dr. Patricia Smith, known as Pat, or Doc. She was a woman of uncompromising integrity. Her grit and strength are the likes of which I have not seen since in woman or man. Her story worth is one worth telling [I recommend Hilary Smith and Pat Smith and the Minh Quy Experience]...a female version of Tom Dooley. I affectionately thought of her as a "bitch on wheels." Her toughness, strength, courage, kindness, and love, plus her taste for whiskey. That fact that she proudly could drink any man, including Col. C, under the table was renown. I remember the times at dinners, military and civilian, around her table was great fun and much laughter. She loved to laugh. She was as devoutly Roman Catholic and as irreverent of any power, save God, as anyone I have ever known.

She ran the hospital with an iron fist and loving heart. Her work was the main source of health care for the indigenous population. The Montagnard could go to the local Vietnamese hospital, but in addition to the barrier of distance, such care was noted for its poor treatment of the native population. I could and did carry on my agricultural work in conjunction with the hospital gardener to grow food in the gardens, which we did to good success. When someone went to the hospital, the whole family came as they were primarily responsible for the feeding and care of the person. The hospital provided what it could from its gardens to supplement.

At Minh Quy I would meet Jeff, a British volunteer, who had come to help. He was as crazy and warm-hearted a man as I ever I knew, and he did put us up to some mischief. He was known for his dangerous runs to get hospital supplies in his brand-new Red Cross Land Rover.

I recall one trip. The hospital needed medical supplies warehoused in Quy Nhơn awaiting air transport, but at an exceptionally low-priority rating. The hospital needed the supplies yesterday. So, one day Jeff and I were going to be heroes and get them by road. Down to Pleiku, across to Quy Nhơn, and back for supper. What could be the problem? Well, we knew enough to know that no one in their right mind would make the trip from Pleiku to Quy Nhơn unless in a tank running full throttle, yet that seemed not to bother us. Well, we did smoke a lot of great weed that day, so maybe our judgment was a little off. A few klicks[11] east of Pleiku, a bullet zipping through our cab brought us back to our senses.

But, I am getting ahead of the story. We had had an uneventful Kon Tum to Pleiku run and that was not unexpected as we made that run regularly without problem, even as we passed through VC territory. But east of Pleiku was all new to us, and we knew it to be dangerous, even mined. But the buses had gone through, so we thought, what the hell? We were not too many kilometers east of Pleiku when I felt and then heard the zip of a hot bullet right past my nose and out Jeff's side door window.

I turned and saw a look of sheer terror on Jeff's face, mirroring, I am sure, what was on mine. It was then that we could hear automatic weapons fire. It was coming from somewhere over a knoll to our right. I was packing a "grease gun[12]," but there was no thought to using it. We stopped, the bullets stopped, and we turned and ran. Once out of range, we laughed until tears, once again dodging death. I learned that day, you do not get to hear the bullet that kills you. Later, in Kon Tum, we counted three bullet holes on the side of the cab. We never tried that again.

And Jeff was so much more sexually adventurous than me. He claimed he got into a vehicle accident when in Saigon. In the car were two French women.

---

[11] kilometers

[12] an M3 sub-machine gun

To settle this unfortunate affair, he claimed the three of them had sex together. I believed him. I knew enough about sex to know about threesomes, but I thought that was only a fantasy. That people even did that, that he did that in real time, a bit of a shock to me. I both admired and was quite jealous of his sexual confidence.

I remember some Saigon night adventures. We would get stoned and walk around until the wee hours, well after curfew. No one was out except for an occasional military police jeep packed with soldiers on patrol, racing down the streets. We would duck into the shadows to let them pass, walk as far as we could in one direction until we turned into another by the sound of gun shots and bullets whizzing ever lower over our heads.

And, one night, a foray into the domains of the sexual underground. What happened was very timid, if truth be told, but the first steps for a sexually recovering Catholic boy. Jeff was enticing me at the end of one of our nightly forays onto the streets to challenge the fates and convinced me to go to a "steam bath."

One of the first things I remember about Saigon was the chatter about the steam baths. There was even one across the street from IVS that everyone, including the women, twitted about. Something about "happy ending" massages. I never paid the subject much mind as a massage in general was not a thing I ever thought of doing. And as for "happy endings," not my thing, and judged it as not being right. But on this night, now one and half years in Vietnam, I said yes. Jeff could be persuasive. I made it clear: no "happy ending." I said it was against my religion. I had a wonderful steam bath, followed by a great massage by a young woman fully dressed Vietnamese style. At the end of the massage, she pointed to my unaroused penis and noted in Vietnamese the word for "small," meaning not erect (I like to think!).

Undulating hand movements indicating her intentions, but I told her no, in Vietnamese. As I got up to dress, in walked a scantily dressed young woman to entice me by gestures rather suggestive into buying a "happy ending." I repeated I would not pay. I figured no pay no play, and I would be out of there.

She left, and then another woman tried to persuade me, and then a parade of five women, each very scantily-clad came dancing in. They flattered me, said I looked like Ho Chi Minh (I was very thin and had a beard) as a sign of respect for me. Still, I refused to pay. Not until they all ran down the hall laughing to Jeff…Jeff the whole time encouraged them not to give up on me. *This must be a slow night*, I was thinking. They got Jeff to pay for it, and to make it end I gave in. They came rushing in and pushed me back on table, touching me all over. My penis was responding even as I still was unsure, and then giving over. I remember Kama Sutra-like images…these women of the night did things to me never done before. I'd never been touched or touched like that before or felt such pleasure.

The oddest part of the experience is that as I orgasmed, a man ran from behind the curtain rushed out with transparent plastic bag in hand and caught my rather abundant sperm in mid-flight. Odd, I thought.

I never did pay Jeff back.

Random Memories of Vietnam, 1967-1969

Here are some collected thoughts that do not have a place elsewhere:

I remember how the Vietnamese who fought the Americans died by the thousands in many battles. Mowed down by superior weaponry and yet, they kept on fighting. They were a warrior culture, skilled in guerrilla techniques, keeping China at bay for centuries. Yet, by temperament, there were a peaceful people. Seemed that when an argument among friends would break out, it was the women who made peace. I may be wrong about that as a cultural thing, though.

After a firefight around Kon Tum, the South Vietnamese army would gather up the enemy dead and pile shredded bodies of Viet Cong and North Vietnamese killed in previous night's attack in the center of Kon Tum's marketplace. The bodies stacked high, like a still picture forever frozen in time in my mind. By the truck loads, shattered bodies were piled high. A warning for all to see if you joined the VC.

From notes to a friend: I have mentioned before that immediately after entering Vietnam, I had a very brief encounter with a Vietnamese male who said, "A nation at war with itself is a nation of spies." As I noted in other notes to you, it was my contact with spies on both sides that saved my life. I was able to travel into the jungle to meet with villagers needing my services. I came back alive, and this was always a mystery to my American counterparts. I think the CIA sent a "deep agent" to befriend me, to check me out. Canadians—you never know whose side they are on!

The CIA? Ford Broncos and International Scouts were the most ubiquitous vehicles for American government workers, and they were very visible in the streets. The CIA used Broncos, usually black in color. If hiding in plain sight was their objective, it seemed not to be the case. My contact with the CIA was casual and periodic. Most of my exchanges took place over dinner in officer quarters. They knew the situation was grim, even as they toed the party line. Always amazed by the shit that came out of the general's and politician's mouths. Was no one listening to them?

I remember R[13], the fastest gun in the West, or should I say the East? After much drinking and demonstrating with an empty revolver, R would initiate a game of "draw." Each man, face to face, about four feet apart... eye to eye. I can still see him looking at me and me at him, my arms spread out at shoulder height, my palms facing each other about a foot apart, his hand on his holstered revolver. The challenge? Clap my hands together, I win. Pistol between hands, he wins. I can still hear the click as he pulled the trigger, his pistol between my hands. R always won the draw. I think it is in the eye. He could see me closing before my muscles could do it... just a fraction of millisecond was all he needed to win every time. Quick reaction time was always key to victory.

I was most impressed with the officer core of the US Army. Many of them knew they were fighting a bogus cause (they would have agreed if Vietnam invaded America, then they would be fighting to oust the invader) and sworn to die fighting for what the commander in chief thought right. Duty above Honor. I wonder about that.

Green: Vietnam is as green as Ireland, I believe. Lush vegetation, fish, rich soil, beautiful beaches, highlands, and one of the largest natural rice growing deltas in the world...the Mekong.

People: the people of the north and a people of the south were related but somewhat different cultures, sharing a common language and heritage. I learned about the cut of clothing and hair on women that distinguished women of the north from women of the south. They

---

[13] a CIA agent

are a beautiful people. Slender with strong bodies. By our standards, most lived a hard life with long hours of hard work in hot sun, showing early on their faces. Their lives were made a little more bearable by the soothing feelings that came from chewing the betel nut.

A friend asked: What country was the nun who was your supervisor from? In my role as team leader for CRS Kon Tum, my supervisor was Sr. Mary. She was from the US. I have attached a copy of her letter of recommendation.

Spring 1969

CRS Kon Tum moved into our downtown digs, comfortably large enough for all of us, and settled into the work. My work was now more administrative, making sure my team got what they needed for day-to-day operations and that no one was feeling overlooked. I was overseeing the unloading and distribution of supplies for refugees and making sure there was no cheating, as well as filling requests for water pumps, seeds, fertilizers, and weed killers for garden projects. I now had "deuce and a half" for the hauling. Fr. Shu, a young priest full of goodness, became my intermediary for tribal needs. Seems I was always in the air, back and forth to Saigon. Most of those trips were unremarkable, except for the couple of incidents that I referenced earlier. Made life interesting, living on an edge. One day blended into the next.

There were some events that stood out. One of the sisters had a motorcycle accident, receiving a significant injury to her ankle. The other driver complained it was her fault. Sr. didn't disagree. I do remember it costing me a lot to settle the matter. One late afternoon, with the sun going down, one of the nurses came to me in a panic. She could not find the urethra of a woman badly in need of release. Not the usual sort of thing that crossed my desk, but what the hell, no one else was around, so I calmed her down and held the light for her to get it done. Up close and for the first time in the light, I could see that female genitals seemed complicated!

On the medical team at Minh Quy was a Maryknoll nun, Sr. Marie. On loan from her Korea assignment, I recall. Always of sunny disposition and a great sense of humor. It seemed wisps of her Irish blond hair were always escaping her headdress, and her energy was so strong. We took a liking to each other. She had great fun poking fun at me and my way to the amusement of the team. She called me "Rab." I loved her. Not in that way, but I think she did flirt a bit. All in all, me and the women were doing all right.

In the background of whatever each day was about, there was the noise of war.

Having too much to drink was a nightly habit now. It was vodka straight up, sometimes half the bottle, to calm the nerves. I remembered my father's alcoholism as I was lying in bed and listening for the guard to walk by my window and give a little whistle. All was OK. Go to sleep. The static on the radiophone was part of my nightly background noise, my connection to the MACV. Col. C made this a requirement for our security.

Suddenly, one night that spring a terrifying noise sounded right out back of our house. The radio was blaring loud enough to wake the dead. "Attack! Take cover!" Awaked in terror from sleep once again. I slept on the ground floor nearest to the entrance, gun by my side. On the first floor there was also Sr. E; her room was at the back of the house beyond the kitchen. Next thing I know, Sr. E is at my door, screaming in terror. I can barely hear her above the noise, her mouth wide open. In the dark, her white nightgown was outlined by the flashing light; she looked so terrified, she glowed white. And yes, she looked quite pretty too, I remember. I hugged her to ground her, and then I was joined by the others who slept on the second floor, and off to the bunker we went. Rockets landed particularly close that night. I still have a piece of one as a memento.

My CRS contract was for 18 months, set to end in 1969. In the spring of 1969, I was coming up on two years in Vietnam, which was my original commitment, Luisa very much on my mind. And I was feeling really stressed out. The intensity of the war was increasing. It was patently clear that unless the US planned to nuke Vietnam, these people were not giving up to the foreigner. I prayed the US would give up so to stop the killing. All this blood unjustly shed.

I remember one afternoon as I was standing in the kitchen, listening to the cook complain about the shockwaves from artillery stopping her bread from rising. I can still see her face looking at me as if it were somehow my fault. I did momentarily feel guilty. What surprised me was that I was unaware of the blasts except as background noise as by now my body and mind were conditioned to the shock. The thought occurred to me as I was coming up on another year in the country that I needed a break.

And I took that vacation with my friend, Mike F. He was classmate from seminary. He asked, and I told him not to come to Vietnam. He did anyhow, with CRS. Although we were working in different programs, our paths crossed often, and many good times were had. The vacation destination was Hong Kong, with the main focus of buying a stereo system… top quality and very inexpensive to send back to the states. Which we did. It was a top of the line eight track, as I recall.

Three memories in particular from Hong Kong stand out.

First: Most of the time we were there we walked, talked, and ate. It was so wonderful to eat and walk the streets and not be afraid.

Second: It was my first exposure to porn. I don't remember how it happened, but Mike and I were following this Chinese person, who said that for some money, he would show us movies…sexy movies. Well, we were not exactly two wild guys on the prowl, but this seemed a safe enough bet for a walk on the wild side. I remember sitting in a small room with him, but the film was of such poor quality, I remember not one image.

Third: Me and the stripper. We were seated at a table that was ring side to the floor show. It was a huge crowd of cheering men and women watching singers and dancers of various performances; the noise was loud. And then came out a surprise to me and Mike. We did not know that the top evening entertaining in Hong Kong was strip tease. Its prominence was a surprise to my puritanical roots.

I watched with due respect and delight as the stripper stripped to fully naked as she erotically danced the stage. I remember her slight body being well formed. Long black hair, very white skin. Very red lips. The erotic ideal. And coming near us on the edge of the stage, she in a split second danced over to Mike. She wrapped herself around him in a most inviting way. I could see his surprise. The crowd began roaring their delight. For me, it always was whenever we were in a bar for western food and a beer that girls talked to me. But bar girls always crowded around him, blond, blued-eyed, and handsome; me, blue eyes, but otherwise dark, reddish, and skinny. Often greeted with "ugly American," referring to my looks as I walked the streets. Maybe sometimes the other meaning as well. So, I thought it normal she chose him as her toy.

I relaxed to enjoy Mike's uncomfortableness as the crowd roared its approval as she moved in sexual ways. Then, as I remember even now in an instant, she leapt off him, and before I could blink, leapt onto my lap. I can still feel the suddenness of her body up against me. With some waves of her hands around my face, she looked me in the eye. I was transfixed. And she grabbed my glasses, quick as a wink. Startled, I can still feel them slipping from my face. After some suggestive moves around my body, she got up and danced backward to the stage, inviting me to follow, with her fingers and lips beckoning me. Next, she ran up on the stage, waving about my glasses, and then proceeded to do a dance with some naughty moves…all of which was a haze to me sitting there stunned. I was a long way from home and not really prepared to play the stud. The crowd was roaring.

Next, I remember that I see her lying on the floor center stage, rubbing my glasses all over with particular attention to her mound, mouth, and breasts. I can still hear the crowd roaring in approval. With her other hand, her middle finger was inviting me on the stage. I resisted. I guess I expected her to dance down and put them back on. But no. The more I resisted, the naughtier things she did with my glasses. My natural high Irish color was now beet red. Encouraged by Mike,

I got up thinking that all I had to do was reach down and get them. But oh no. Stupid me, this is a dance for which I was unprepared. Every time I reached down; she snatched my glasses away. And I had quick reflexes. Then, I saw her free hand motioning for me to get between her open legs. I knew enough about sex to get the drift of her performance expectations and once again, I denied as I reached down to get them. Quicker reflexes than me. She placed them right over her pubis and invited me to get down on my knees between her legs and get them with my teeth. I learnt that night that whatever the nature of my sexuality, being a Sub was not my thing. But to get this done and to be a good sport, I became her "bitch," as they say. And hearing the roar in approval, I had to end it. I did it. My mouth watered as I saw and felt her silky fur on my lips. I quickly returned to my seat, waving at the crowd my glasses, trying to look the victor. They roared. Quite an introduction to cunnilingus!

The next night, we were at a working dinner in a very upscale hotel restaurant with senior CRS leadership. They were from New York, touring the region. They were wanting to get our input on Vietnam. We were seated high up, looking over city at the back of the room.

After work was done, we wanted to enjoy the floor show again. I turned to look, and guess who was up on stage, doing her thing. I was instantly afraid she would see me. Wouldn't look good to have the stripper come rushing off the stage in front of senior brass. I felt silly for the thought that she would even remember me. Oddly, as I watched her beautiful show, I noted that no unsuspecting male was lured onto the stage. And so, I wondered, maybe she did have a memory of me. A one off. Me and the stripper had a moment in time.

Upon return from Hong Kong, my brother, Garry, wrote me to say he was to marry and asked would I come home for it. Also, Lou, my physician priest friend, mentioned that his ordination was at the end of June. Marie said she was going. It seemed time to come home and evaluate whether I had it in me to return to Vietnam.

My two years up, I returned to the Canada in June 1969. I dealt with what I came home to attend to, and I felt very conflicted about returning to Vietnam. I felt like I was abandoning my team just as things were getting worse. I was underweight (still in recovery from murine typhus) and on the verge of becoming an alcoholic. In my gut, I knew my time in Vietnam was done. I gave what I could, and it was time to come home.

In July of 1969, after much careful consideration, I made the decision not to return. The call to family and friends brought me home, but most particularly, my deep and lasting love, Luisa, was the priority.

My vision quest was done…enough was enough. Now, it was time to be with her[14].

---

[14] Our story, the unpublished *Jan and Luisa: Monk and Contessa*

Civilian Vietnam War Veteran

Unknown to me at the time of Tet '68, the USA State Department sent to my parents a Missing in Action (MIA) letter. For the shock of that letter to my mother Theresa, I sometimes wished I never left the farm.

Some years ago, I acknowledged to myself that I am a Civilian Vietnam War Veteran. This was the beginning of my being able to tell the story of my time in war. I find it of great concern, now some 34 years later, that America has been drawn into another guerrilla war. There is something about that war now so long ago that feels strangely like Bush's war on terrorism. It is a sense of déjà vu, of repeating old errors in war and peace that compels me to write about the Age of Terrorism that is upon us. Perhaps I survived to author this story in the hopes of an Age of Peace.

—February 1, 2003

Epilogue

In journal notes of January 2005, I lament now that so many years later, as I read my reflections of January 10, 1968, how I am once again in war so close to home. I write these words not fifty miles from New York City, a large scar signaling the next stage in a war started centuries ago. It seems we are paying the price for getting into the middle toppling Iranian democracy some half century ago. Imagine if we had not done that. Instead, there is no talk of peace between the warring factions, as each side believes they are winning, and the desire for war is growing among masses on either side.

In my gut, I have the same kind of tightness of fall '67, and my nightmares of those times come back to haunt me. I pray I project my past onto the future.

I think not as I read the tea leaves in 2021 and reread my reflections of my times past in war. I look out my window and perceive our situation to be exponentially worse than it was in 2005. Newton's laws of motion. Without a global intervention, humanity is on the path to great destruction in the terrors of war and warming unbounded. Most people seem to be caught in a trance...not wanting to believe that we live in such a treacherous time. And they feel powerless to change what at this time is the inevitability of the Age of Catastrophe. We are blinded by money and power and are not seeing the possibility of an Age of Peace, even as our great books call for it.

From the terror of January 10, 1968, a night so long ago, a dream has arisen: From human civilization founded on war to human civilization founded on justice. True justice is love manifested as right action.

A dream is for humanity to stand billions strong to occupy one virtual conscious space, the energy focused and committed to moving huge steps forward in human development. It is a matter of numbers. In one voice, an awakening global consciousness committed to voting for leaders from every people tribe, nation, and state to build a global civilization living in an age of peace ruled by justice.

End War + End Warming = Age of Peace

We live in a time when this can be done. It is no different from selling Fords.

AgeofPeace2050.com is a vision and a blueprint.

This is my legacy.

June 10, 2021

JanStephen James Cavanaugh, PhD

"It isn't enough to talk about peace.

One must believe in it.

And it isn't enough to believe in it.

One must work at it"

Elanor Roosevelt

And then vote for it. jsjc

August 4, 1969

Dear Mr. & Mrs. Cavanaugh,

Here are a couple of pictures of your son taken in front of CRS the day he left Saigon.

I want you to know that I consider Jan one of the finest young men it has ever been my good fortune to meet.

He was an inspiration to all of us here in CRS. You are truly blessed.

Sincerely,

Edmund J. Conway

Jan Stephen Cavanaugh, Saigon, 1968

JAN CAVANAUGH

Barrie Man Serving In Saigon With Catholic Relief Service

SAIGON — Jan Cavanaugh son of Mr. and Mrs. Leo J. Cavanaugh of Melrose Ave., Barrie, has been appointed to duties here with Catholic Relief Services, overseas aid agency of American Catholics, as a member of the agency's Refugee Rehabilitation program. Mr. Cavanaugh joined CRS on May 98 for an 18-month tour after working one year Service in Vietnam's beleaguered Central Highlands. While with IVS, he was an agricultural and administrative advisor at a Montagnard training center near Kontum.

At 24, Cavanaugh is the youngest member of the new CRS project staff. He is now tentatively assigned to Pleiku Province, also in the Central Highlands, as leader of a five-man team that will be sent there shortly.

Mr. Cavanaugh, a graduate of St. Joseph's High school, Barrie, received his bachelor of arts degree in philosophy from Glen Ellyn College, Glen Ellyn, Ill. He has also done graduate work in theology at the University of San Francisco.

CLINICAL RECORD COVER SHEET
(AR 40-400)

1. ADMISSION NOTES	2. WARD	3. TYPE OF CASE	4. LAST NAME—FIRST NAME—MIDDLE INITIAL
1200	3	☒ DIS ☐ INJ ☐ SC	CAVANAUGH, Jan B.

5. SEX	6. RELIGION	7. PREV. ADM.	8. REGISTER NO.	9. SERVICE NO.	10. GRADE
M	C	☐ YES ☒ NO	14440		

11. RATING OR DSGN	12. DEPARTMENT	13. ORGANIZATION AND BRANCH OF SERVICE	14. FLYING STATUS
		US Civ Empl/USA	

No next of kin or N

15. NAME AND ADDRESS OF EMERGENCY ADDRESSEE	16. AGE	17. RACE	18. LENGTH OF SERVICE	19. DATE OF ADMISSION
(redacted)	24	Cau	—	5 Feb 68

20. SOURCE OF ADMISSION: AR40-3, para 16a

NOTE: Enter flying status for AF Military Personnel only. For Civilians, etc., show type (Dep. of EM, etc.) in space 13.

21. ADMITTING OFFICER	22. CONTINUATION OF ITEMS 13 AND 20
D.O.B. 10 Jan 43 — J.M. REED CPT, MC	(13)AO 96499

23. DIAGNOSES (See instructions for recording as shown on reverse side. Include all required related data)

CAVANAUGH JAN # 8039-013
I vs

REGISTER OR UNIT NO. — WARD NO. OPD — ☒ AMBULATORY
REQUESTED BY AND DATE: REED — DATE AND TIME COLLECTED: 5 Feb 65
CLINICAL DATA: High fevers; Exanthematous rash of trunk. Dx at V.N Hospital as having Typhoid Fever.
EXAMINATION REQUESTED: Anti-Body Titer S. Typhosa

24. RESULT:
Sera dtd 5 Feb and 13 Feb 68 tested by CF with Murine Typhus antigen. Titers demonstrated indicate a Murine Typhus infection.

	Titer (reciprocal)
5 Feb	8
13 Feb	64

ROBERT M. MCKINNEY
MSC
DATE OF REPORT: 29 FEB — MICROBIOLOGY DEPT.
NAME OF MEDICAL FACILITY: 17th Field Hospital

62-2-8

PHYSICAL PROFILE

TYPE	SERIAL					SUFFIX					
	P	U	L	H	E	S	R	T	D	G	N
PREVIOUS											
REVISED											

☐ PROFILE IS UNCHANGED

27. DAYS DURATION THIS FACILITY
ALL 15 IN HOSPITAL OR INFIRMARY 15 SUBSISTING ELSEWHERE ___ QUARTERS OR DISPENSARY ___ LEAVE ___ OTHER ___

28. NATURE OF DISPOSITION	29. DATE OF DISPOSITION
Discharged from hospital	21 February 68

30. SIGNATURE OF ATTENDING PHYSICIAN: S/PAUL J. REED CPT, MC
31. SIGNATURE OF REGISTRAR OR MEDICAL RECORDS OFFICER

32. NAME AND LOCATION OF MEDICAL TREATMENT FACILITY	33. REGISTER NUMBER
17TH FIELD HOSPITAL, APO 26248	14440

DA FORM 8-275-3 (4 PART) 1 JUL 62 — REPLACES DD FORM 481-3, 1 SEP 52, EXISTING SUPPLIES OF WHICH WILL BE ISSUED AND USED UNTIL 1 JUL 63 UNLESS SOONER EXHAUSTED.

THE UNIVERSITY OF CONNECTICUT   OFFICE OF PLACEMENT AND CAREER PLANNING
                              Box U-51
                              Storrs, Conn. 06268

_Jan Stephan Cavanaugh_____ has filed with this office and has established a set of credentials including written references. Your recommendation will become part of the file and will be treated as a confidential statement, but may be shown to the candidate by the Placement Office staff if the candidate requests.

Your statement should indicate your support of this person and include such points as, how long and in what capacity you have known him or her and the quality of work done under your direction. Please include your assessment of the candidate's potential for professional advancement as well as any personality traits such as creativity, maturity and judgment, desire for innovation, and leadership potential you have observed.

Thank you for your assistance and cooperation in completing and returning this evaluation as soon as possible. Please type or print in ink to facilitate machine reproduction.

It gives me great pleasure to recommend Jan S. Cavanaugh whom I have known since 1967, when I first became acquainted with Mr. Cavanaugh in Viet Nam where we were both on staff of Catholic Relief Services - Viet Nam. Mr. Cavanaugh was Team Leader of the CRS-USAID Team in Kontum Province in the western mountainous region of VN boardering Laos, and was responsible administratively to me in my capacity of Coordinator of Medical Services and supervisor to Mr. Cavanaugh.

I was based in Saigon or Cam Ranh Bay and could visit Kontum at infrequent intervals. The success of the project under Mr. Cavanaugh's direction can be attributed almost wholly to his organizational and administrative abilities, his conceptual skills, his energy, dedication and perseverance, as well as a considerable degree of personal bravery and selflessness.

Mr. Cavanaugh's team comprised two registered nurses, a registered laboratory technologist, and a nutritionist, all USA citizens; his own expertise was in the area of community and social developments.

The Kontum CRS-USAID Team was located in one of the most isolated and hazardous war areas. It administered chiefly to the Mongagnard aboriginals, a minority group rather neglected over the years of French and Vietnamese bureaucracy, and frequently dislocated by the sporadic fighting in their area.

In addition to his fluency in Vietnamese, a difficult tonal language, Mr. Cavanaugh developed marked ability to use the three main Montagnard tongues, which are basically different from Vietnamese.

Under Mr. Cavanaugh's direction, the Montagnard project had three main activities: first, in conjunction with the small hospital started and operated by Dr. Patricia Smith of Seattle, Washington, and the Provincial Hospital, in Kontum, to supplement training in basic nursing and administration, and to set up laboratory techniques with selected Montagnards as an aid to Dr. Smith and the medical staff of the Provincial Hospital in diagnosis of the principal medical ailments among the Montagnards: anemia, liver, and intestinal infections; during Mr. Cavanaugh's tenure, the USA medical technologist developed a simple laboratory procedures manual in Binar, one of the Montagnard tongues;

Mary T. McDonough
Name (Printed or typed)   The candidate has (not) been made aware of the contents of
Deputy Executive Director-Business & Personnel   this statement.
Official Position
The American Nurses' Association
Institution   Signature
2420 Pershing Road, Kansas City, Missouri
Location   Date Written

Rev. 7/72

ORIGINAL RELEASED
To Candidate on 6-15-81

this was a revolutionary innovation, both because little of the Montagnard languages had been commited to writing, and because of the scientific aspect of this attempt; secondly, also in conjunction with the Smith Hospital, the nutritionist developed simple recipes using available donated commodities, which were acceptable to the Montagnard dietary culture, and which helped introduce them to an understanding of nutritional requirements (many of the infants died young from nutritional deficiencies or related severe anemia and worm infestation); the third activity centered on development or improvement of farming and animal husbandry and seed and animal credit banks, and sanitary facilities.

This latter area was Mr. Cavanaugh's particular endeavor, in addition to his overall administrative responsibility for the Team. He had remarkable success in working with a rather primitive, but intelligent group, and by his own hard work, sensitivity and respect in his dealings with the Montagnards, he inspired initiative and industry, and developed with them several outstanding and successful projects, which promised to be self sustaining, on American withdrawal; in his relations with the American Team, he manifested remarkable leadership in developing an excellent espirit-de-corps, in providing a climate which allowed each Team member to propose worthwhile projects and to collaborate successfully with the Montagnards in their own self development. Mr. Cavanaugh's Team was probably one of the hardest working and most unified Teams among the CRS-USAID Teams in VN. This cohesion and high productivity must be attributed to Mr. Cavanaugh's ability to draw out potential in individuals, to teach and counsel, but not crowd, and in the very hazardous war-time atmosphere, to provide support and a feeling of security and accomplishment.

I did have to counsel Mr. Cavanaugh to budget his own stamina and to take required rest; however, I believe that he ordinarily strikes a balance between work and relaxation, but circumstances in Viet Nam in 1967-68 did not allow this balance.

In his dealings with the United States Government representatives, both lay and military, and the representatives of the Government Viet Nam, Mr. Cavanaugh displayed tact, good judgment and impartiality, and controlled patience in the face of many frustrations occasioned by war, difficult logistics, overlapping lines of authority, and bureaucratic intransigence, and the like.

I have written at length to attempt to convey that Mr. Cavanaugh is a fine and good man in every sense of the word and an outstanding administrator, teacher, and counsellor. I believe he will bring to whatever job he undertakes a high degree of intelligence, sensitivity, commitment and success.

MTM:of

www.ingramcontent.com/pod-product-compliance
Lightning Source LLC
Chambersburg PA
CBHW071856070526
44583CB00016B/1721